GREAT TASTES

BAKING

D1373831

First published in 2009 by Bay Books, an imprint of Murdoch Books Pty Limited
This edition published in 2010.

Murdoch Books Australia
Pier 8/9
23 Hickson Road
Millers Point NSW 2000
Phone: +61 (0) 2 8220 2000
Fax: +61 (0) 2 8220 2558
www.murdochbooks.com.au

Murdoch Books UK Limited
Erico House, 6th Floor
93–99 Upper Richmond Road
Putney, London SW15 2TG
Phone: +44 (0) 20 8785 5995
Fax: +44 (0) 20 8785 5985
www.murdochbooks.co.uk

Chief Executive: Juliet Rogers
Publishing Director: Kay Scarlett
Publisher: Lynn Lewis
Senior Designer: Heather Menzies
Designer: Wendy Inkster
Production: Kita George

ISBN: 9780681657724

PRINTED IN CHINA

IMPORTANT: Those who might be at risk from the effects of salmonella poisoning (the elderly, pregnant women, young children and those suffering from immune deficiency diseases) should consult their doctor with any concerns about eating raw eggs.

OVEN GUIDE: You may find cooking times vary depending on the oven you are using. For fan-forced ovens, as a general rule, set the oven temperature to 20°C (35°F) lower than indicated in the recipe.

GREAT TASTES

BAKING

More than 120 easy recipes for every day

bay books

CONTENTS

BREAD

BREADS BASICS

Throughout the culinary world, bread is a regarded as a symbol of sustenance, and is eaten at all times of the day. There is nothing better than good bread fresh from the oven, with its heady aroma, crisp golden crust and soft, light crumb. Slathered with butter while it's still warm, dipped in olive oil, used for sandwiches or to mop up a stew or soup, bread is undeniably a vital and enjoyable part of our everyday life.

Yeast breads

We make breads using commercial yeast (either fresh or dried) or with chemical raising agents such as baking powder. Yeast is used to leaven a wide range of different breads, from a basic loaf to pizza bases. The dough may be enriched with eggs and butter, sweetened with sugar and honey and enhanced with chocolate, spices, herbs, nuts, seeds and cheese, to name a few.

- When adding water to yeast (or a yeast and flour mixture), warm it first until tepid or hand hot. Do not use water that is too hot to touch or it will kill the yeast.

- If dissolving yeast first, leave it in a warm place for at least 10 minutes, or until a good foam appears on the surface. If it does not foam, the yeast is dead and you will have to start again with a new batch.

- If mixing dough by hand, use a wooden spoon to bring the ingredients together. The dough should feel sticky when it first comes together. If it feels dry, add a little more water, a tablespoon at a time.

- If using an electric stand mixer always use the dough attachment, unless otherwise specified. Stand the mixer well away from the edge of the work surface because it may move as it is mixing the dough.

- Always start with the electric mixer on its lowest setting to first mix the ingredients, then increase the speed to medium to knead the dough.

- When leaving dough to rise, use a large bowl at least twice the size of the dough so it has plenty of room to expand.

- Lightly oil both the bowl and the surface of the dough before leaving the dough to rise. The dough should be covered with plastic wrap to prevent it forming a skin, which prevents it rising properly.

- To test if a dough has risen sufficiently, press a finger into the surface. The fingerprint should remain indented and should not spring back.

- Draughts can cause dough to deflate, so make sure the room is draught-free. Doughs will rise too fast if the room is overly hot, which will give an unpleasant smell and flavour to the bread. If this happens, deflate the dough and leave to rise again in a cool place (for at least 1 hour to develop flavour).

- Lightly flour the work surface before shaping the dough.

- If leaving bread dough overnight in the refrigerator, allow time for it to return to room temperature so it can begin to rise. This should take 45–60 minutes.

- Always grease the tin with spray oil or melted butter. Baking trays should be lightly greased or dusted with flour.

- When pressing dough into a tin it should reach to 1.5 cm (½ inch) below the top of the tin. After rising, the centre of the dough should protrude about 2.5 cm (1 inch) above the top of the tin. The dough is then ready to be baked.

- Never open the oven door during the first half of the total baking time or the bread can collapse. If you do need to turn the bread to get even browning, do this after the halfway point.

- To test if a bread is cooked, gently remove it from the tray or tin and tap it on the bottom — it should sound hollow. If it doesn't, return it to the oven for a further 5 minutes, then test again.

- Store bread in a paper or cloth bag for up to 24 hours in a cool place. Do not refrigerate bread as this makes it become stale more quickly. If keeping bread longer, store in a plastic bag or a zip lock bag.

- To freeze bread, wrap it in plastic wrap and then place inside a freezer bag. Defrost to room temperature before use. Bread that is allowed to defrost slowly, at room temperature, will retain its freshness for longer.

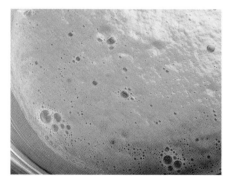

Leave the yeast mixture in a warm place until well risen and foamy.

To knead, push the dough away from you with the heel of your hand.

Leave covered, in a warm place until the dough has doubled in size.

Mysteries of yeast solved

Working with yeast, probably the most important ingredient in bread, is not as difficult as you may think. Yeast is available dried or fresh. Dried yeast, generally comes in a box containing 7 g (¼ oz) sachets, one of which is enough for a standard loaf. Fresh yeast, has quite a short storage life. About 15 g (½ oz) of fresh yeast is equivalent to a 7 g (¼ oz) sachet of dried yeast.

Types of flour

The type and quality of flour you use is vital. The correct flour makes a big difference to the quality of bread. Some of the recipes call for the use of flour that is labelled as bread flour. This is high in protein and will form gluten, which helps the bread rise well and bake into a light airy loaf with a good crust. For most breads, if you use a regular flour the loaf will not rise well, gluten will not form and the loaf will be heavy and dense.

Kneading the dough

The dough is then formed into a ball on a lightly floured surface and kneaded. Don't be tempted to cut short the kneading time as it affects the texture of the finished bread. Kneading distributes the yeast evenly throughout the dough and allows the flour's protein to develop into gluten. Gluten gives the dough elasticity, strength and the ability to expand, as it traps the carbon dioxide gas created by the yeast and this allows the bread to rise. The kneading action is simple and it's quite easy to get into a rhythm. Hold one end of the dough down with one hand, and stretch it away from you with the other hand. Then fold the dough back together, make a quarter turn and repeat the action. Knead for 10 minutes, or until smooth and elastic.

Punching down

After proving, punch down the dough to expel the air, and knead again for 1 minute, or until smooth. The dough is now ready for shaping. Shape the loaf to fit into the prepared tin, placing it in with any seam at the base. Cover with plastic wrap or a damp tea towel (dish towel) and place the tin in a warm, draught-free place until the dough is well risen and doubled in size. This will take about 45–60 minutes. This is the final rise for the dough.

Storage

Home-baked bread is best eaten on the day of baking, but it can be wrapped and frozen for up to 3 months. When required, thaw at room temperature, then refresh in a 180°C (350°F/Gas 4) oven for 10 minutes.

What went wrong

DEAD: If your yeast mixture has not risen and is not frothy, the yeast is dead. If this happens, you will have to throw away the mixture and start again. Take care when measuring the yeast. The temperature of the water should be tepid, not too warm, or you may kill the yeast. If using dry yeast, check the expiry date on the back of the packet before you start.

STRONG SMELL AND TASTE OF YEAST: If there is a strong smell and taste of yeast, the bread was undercooked or there was too much yeast used in proportion to the amount of flour.

LOAF DIDN'T RISE OR ROSE POORLY: If the loaf didn't rise or rose poorly, the yeast was old or dead. The liquid may have been too hot and killed the yeast. The yeast may have worked itself out too early by being placed to rise in a spot that was too warm. It may have been left too long to prove.

LOAF OVER-RISEN AND PUFFY: If there are large holes in the loaf and it has risen too much and is puffy, the dough may have been insufficiently kneaded during the first kneading stage. The rising time for the dough may have too long, or the dough may not have been correctly knocked backed before shaping the loaf.

LOAF AND CRUMB CRUST SEPARATE: If the crumb and crust separate from one another, the bread dough was not properly knocked back before shaping the loaf.

LOAF ROSE UNEVENLY: If the loaf rises unevenly, or is cracked along one side, the oven temperature was uneven or the bread was not placed in the centre of the oven or was too close to the heating elements. The baking tin used may have been too small.

LOAF HAS AN UNEVEN COLOUR: If the bread is unevenly coloured, the oven temperature was uneven, too high or the bread was placed too low in the oven. A hard crust forms if the dough is not covered during the rising stage, allowing the surface to dry out and thus form a crust.

Perfect: Good even crumb; bread has risen evenly and sounds hollow when tapped.

Overcooked: Too dark, cracked on top and a dry crumb.

Undercooked: Damp crumb, sticky and the crust is soft and pale.

SIMPLE WHITE BREAD

**MAKES ONE 25 CM (10 INCH)
OVAL LOAF**

2½ teaspoons (7 g) instant dried yeast

1 teaspoon caster (superfine) sugar

450 g (1 lb/3⅔ cups) white bread
(strong) flour

1   Sprinkle the yeast and sugar over 150 ml (5 fl oz) warm water in a small bowl. Stir to dissolve the sugar, then leave in a draught-free place for 10 minutes, or until the yeast is foamy.

2   Combine the flour and 2 teaspoons salt in the bowl of an electric mixer with a dough hook attachment and make a well in the centre. Add another 150 ml (5 fl oz) warm water to the yeast mixture, then pour the mixture into the well. With the mixer set to the lowest speed, mix for 2 minutes, or until a dough forms. Increase the speed to medium and knead the dough for another 10 minutes, or until it is smooth and elastic. Alternatively, mix the dough by hand using a wooden spoon, then turn out onto a floured work surface and knead for 10 minutes, or until smooth and elastic.

3   Grease a large bowl with oil, then transfer the dough to the bowl, turning the dough to coat in the oil. Cover with plastic wrap and leave to rise in a draught-free place for 1–1½ hours, or until the dough has doubled in size.

4   Knock back the dough by punching it gently, then turn out onto a lightly floured work surface. Shape into a rounded oval and transfer to a greased baking tray. Cover loosely with a damp cloth and leave for 30 minutes, or until doubled in size. Meanwhile, preheat the oven to 190°C (375°F/Gas 5).

5   Using a sharp knife, make three diagonal slashes, about 4 cm (1½ inches) apart, on the top of the loaf. Bake the loaf for 40 minutes, or until it sounds hollow when tapped on the base. Transfer to a wire rack to cool completely.

Note: Because home-baked bread has no preservatives, it is best eaten on the day of baking; otherwise, use it for toast. Bread can be tightly wrapped and frozen for up to 3 months.

PUMPERNICKEL ROLLS

MAKES 12 LUNCH ROLLS OR 16 DINNER ROLLS

90 g (3¼ oz/¼ cup) molasses
30 g (1 oz) butter
1 tablespoon (12 g) instant dried yeast
30 g (1 oz/¼ cup) unsweetened cocoa powder
1 tablespoon soft brown sugar
1½ tablespoons caraway seeds
2 teaspoons fennel seeds
300 g (10½ oz/3 cups) rye flour, plus extra for dusting
375 g (13 oz/3 cups) white bread (strong) flour

1 Heat 500 ml (17 fl oz/2 cups) water, the molasses and butter in a small saucepan over low heat until the butter has melted.

2 Combine the yeast, cocoa powder, sugar, caraway seeds, fennel seeds, 200 g (7 oz/2 cups) of rye flour and 1 teaspoon salt in the bowl of an electric mixer with a dough hook attachment. Pour in butter mixture and, with the mixer set to lowest speed, mix until the ingredients are incorporated, scraping down the bowl as necessary. Add remaining rye flour and mix 2 minutes. Add bread flour, 60 g (2 ¼oz/½ cup) at a time, mixing to form a soft dough. Increase speed to medium and knead 5 minutes, or until the dough is smooth and elastic. Or, mix dough by hand using a wooden spoon. Turn out onto a floured surface. Knead 5 minutes, or until smooth and elastic.

3 Grease a large bowl with oil, then transfer the dough to the bowl, turning the dough to coat in the oil. Cover with

plastic wrap and leave to rise in a draught-free place for 45–60 minutes, or until the dough has doubled in size.

4 Knock back the dough by punching it gently, then turn out onto a floured work surface and divide into 12 equal portions (or 16 if making dinner rolls). Shape each piece into a round, then gently roll to form an oval shape. Transfer the rolls to greased baking trays and dust the tops with extra rye flour. Using a sharp, lightly floured knife, make a 1 cm (½ inch) deep cut across the top of each roll. Cover with a damp cloth and leave for 45 minutes, or until doubled in size. Meanwhile, preheat the oven to 180°C (350°F/Gas 4).

5 Bake the rolls for 35 minutes (or 25–30 minutes for the dinner rolls), or until they sound hollow when tapped on the base. Transfer to a wire rack to cool. Serve the rolls with cheese, olives, smoked salmon and dill pickles.

SUNFLOWER BREAD

SERVES 6–8

155 g (5 oz/1¼ cups) self-raising flour

1 tablespoon caster sugar

2 teaspoons baking powder

1 teaspoon salt

110 g (3½ oz/¾ cup) fine polenta

60 g (2 oz/½ cup) grated cheddar cheese

2 tablespoons chopped flat-leaf (Italian) parsley

1 teaspoon dried oregano

2 eggs

250 ml (8 fl oz/1 cup) milk

80 ml (2¾ fl oz/⅓ cup) sunflower oil

2 tablespoons sunflower seeds

1 **Preheat the oven** to 180°C (350°F/Gas 4). Grease one 20 x 10 cm (8 x 4 inch) loaf tin and line the base with baking paper.

2 **Sift the flour,** sugar, baking powder and salt into a large bowl. Add the polenta, cheddar cheese, parsley and oregano.

3 **Combine the eggs,** milk and oil and pour onto the dry ingredients. Stir until combined.

4 **Pour into the tin** and sprinkle with the sunflower seeds. Bake for 45 minutes, or until a skewer inserted in the centre comes out clean.

WHITE DINNER ROLLS

MAKES 12

1 teaspoon dried yeast
½ teaspoon caster sugar
250 g (8 oz/ 2 cups) plain flour
½ teaspoon salt
1 tablespoon dried whole milk powder
2 teaspoons caster sugar, extra
1½ tablespoon milk
poppy seeds, sesame seeds, caraway seeds, sea salt flakes or plain flour, to decorate

1 Combine the yeast, sugar and 60 ml (2 fl oz/¼ cup) of warm water in a bowl. Cover and set aside in a warm place for 10 minutes, or until frothy.

2 Mix the flour, salt, milk powder and extra sugar in a bowl. Make a well in the centre and pour in the oil, 125 ml (4 fl oz/½ cup of warm water and the frothy yeast. Mix to a soft dough and knead for 10 minutes, or until smooth and elastic. Add a little extra flour if needed. Place in a lightly oiled bowl, cover loosely with greased plastic wrap and leave in a warm place for 1 hour, or until doubled in size.

3 Punch down, knead for 1 minute and divide into twelve. To shape into spirals, roll each portion into a 30 cm (12 inch) rope, coil tightly and tuck under the end to seal. To shape into knots, tie each rope; or shape into ovals and leave plain or slash diagonally.

4 Place apart on lightly greased trays and cover loosely with a damp team towel (dish towel). Leave to rise for 20 minutes.

5 Preheat the oven to 180°C (350°F/Gas 4). Brush with the milk and then sprinkle with your choice of seeds, sea salt flakes or plain flour topping. Bake for 15–20 minutes, or until browned.

WALNUT AND CHEDDAR SODA BREAD

MAKES ONE 20 CM (8 INCH) ROUND LOAF

250 g (9 oz/2 cups) plain (all-purpose) flour

225 g (8 oz/1½ cups) wholemeal (whole-wheat) flour

1 tablespoon baking powder

1 teaspoon bicarbonate of soda (baking soda)

1 tablespoon soft brown sugar

60 g (2¼ oz/½ cup) walnut pieces, chopped

175 g (6 oz/1½ cups) grated mature cheddar cheese

40 g (1½ oz) butter, melted and cooled

2 eggs, lightly beaten

250 ml (9 fl oz/1 cup) buttermilk

1   **Preheat the oven** to 180°C (350°F/Gas 4). Line a baking tray with baking paper.

2   **Sift the flours,** baking powder and bicarbonate of soda into a large bowl (tip any husks from the wholemeal flour left in the sieve back into the mixture). Stir in the sugar, walnuts and cheese. Make a well in the centre. Combine the butter, eggs and buttermilk in a bowl and pour into the well. Stir with a wooden spoon until a soft dough forms, then turn out onto a lightly floured work surface. Using lightly floured hands, knead briefly just until smooth, then shape the dough into a 20 cm (8 inch) round. Transfer to the baking tray.

3   **Using a sharp,** lightly floured knife, cut a 1 cm (½ inch) deep cross into the top of the loaf. Bake for 30–40 minutes, or until golden.

Note: For a variation, replace the cheddar cheese with 100 g (3 oz/½ cup) chopped dried pear and 1 teaspoon aniseed. Bake as above and serve warm, with cheese.

PARMESAN GRISSINI

MAKES 32

1 teaspoon (3 g) instant dried yeast

a pinch of caster (superfine) sugar

1 tablespoon extra virgin olive oil

250 g (9 oz/2 cups) white bread (strong) flour

60 g (2¼ oz/⅔ cup) grated parmesan cheese

1 Sprinkle the yeast and sugar over 170 ml (5½ fl oz/⅔ cup) warm water in a small bowl. Stir to dissolve the sugar, then leave in a draught-free place for 10 minutes, or until the yeast is foamy. Stir in the olive oil.

2 Put the flour in a large bowl, add the parmesan and 1 teaspoon salt and stir to combine well. Pour in the yeast mixture and stir until a dough forms. Turn the dough out onto a lightly floured work surface and knead for 5 minutes, or until the dough is smooth and elastic.

3 Grease a large bowl with oil, then transfer the dough to the bowl, turning the dough to coat in the oil. Cover with plastic wrap and leave to rise in a draught-free place for 1 hour, or until the dough has doubled in size.

4 Preheat the oven to 200°C (400°F/Gas 6). Lightly grease two baking trays. Knock back the dough by punching it gently, then turn out onto a floured work surface and cut in half. Roll out one piece of dough to form a 20 x 16 cm (8 x 6 ¼ inch) rectangle, then cut into sixteen 1 cm (½ inch) wide strips. Using your hands, gently roll each strip to form a 22–24 cm (8½–9½ inch) long stick, then place on the baking tray. Repeat for the second piece of dough. Bake for 17–20 minutes, or until golden and crisp, swapping the trays halfway through to ensure even cooking. Transfer to a wire rack to cool.

5 Grissini will keep, stored in an airtight container, for up to 7 days. Re-crisp in a 180°C (350°F/Gas 4) oven for 5 minutes if they become soft.

CHEESE AND HERB PULL-APART LOAF

MAKES ONE 20 CM (8 INCH) ROUND LOAF

250 g (9 oz/2 cups) plain (all-purpose) flour

225 g (8 oz/1½ cups) wholemeal (whole-wheat) flour

1 tablespoon baking powder

1 teaspoon bicarbonate of soda (baking soda)

1 tablespoon soft brown sugar

60 g (2¼ oz/½ cup) walnut pieces, chopped

175 g (6 oz/1½ cups) grated mature cheddar cheese

40 g (1½ oz) butter, melted and cooled

2 eggs, lightly beaten

250 ml (9 fl oz/1 cup) buttermilk

1 **Preheat the oven** to 180°C (350°F/Gas 4). Line a baking tray with baking paper.

2 **Sift the flours,** baking powder and bicarbonate of soda into a large bowl (tip any husks from the wholemeal flour left in the sieve back into the mixture). Stir in the sugar, walnuts and cheese. Make a well in the centre. Combine the butter, eggs and buttermilk in a bowl and pour into the well. Stir with a wooden spoon until a soft dough forms, then turn out onto a lightly floured work surface. With lightly floured hands, knead briefly just until smooth, then shape the dough into a 20 cm (8 inch) round. Transfer to the baking tray.

3 **Using a sharp,** lightly floured knife, cut a 1 cm (½ inch) deep cross into the top of the loaf. Bake for 30–40 minutes, or until golden.

Note: For a variation, replace the cheddar cheese with 100 g (3½ oz/½ cup) chopped dried pear and 1 teaspoon aniseed. Bake as above and serve warm, with cheese.

RICOTTA AND DILL BUNS

MAKES 8

7 g (¼ oz) dried yeast
1½ teaspoon caster sugar
250 g (8 oz) ricotta cheese
30 g (1 oz) butter, softened
¼ small onion, grated
¼ teaspoon bicarbonate of soda
1 egg
465 g (14½ oz/3¾ cups) plain flour
2 tablespoons chopped dill

1 **Combine the yeast,** sugar and 60 ml (2 fl oz/¼ cup) of warm water in a bowl. Cover and set aside in a warm place for 10 minutes, or until frothy.

2 **Put the ricotta,** butter, onion, bicarbonate of soda and egg in a food processor with 1 teaspoon of salt and process until smooth. Add the frothy yeast and 375 g (12 oz/3 cups) of the flour. Add the remaining flour and mix to a smooth dough. Turn out the dough onto a floured surface and knead for 6–8 minutes, or until smooth. Add dill during the last minute of kneading. Place in a lightly oiled bowl, cover loosely with greased plastic wrap and leave in a warm place for 1 hour, or until doubled in size.

3 **Lightly grease** one 20 x 30 cm (8 x 12 inch) tray.

4 **Punch down** the dough and divide into 8 pieces. Form into rounds and place on the tray. Make 2 slashes on each bun. Cover loosely with a damp team towel (dish towel). Leave to rise for 30 minutes.

5 **Preheat the oven** to 180°C (350°F/Gas 4). Bake the buns for 40–45 minutes, or until golden. Check after 20 minutes and reduce the oven to warm 170°C (325°F/Gas 3) if they are too brown.

ZUCCHINI AND OLIVE BREAD

MAKES 6–8

150 g (5 oz/1 cup) finely grated zucchini (courgettes)

250 g (8 oz/2 cups) self-raising flour

1 teaspoon baking powder

1 teaspoon salt

1 teaspoon caster sugar

125 g (4 oz/1 cup) grated cheddar cheese

2 tablespoons chopped chives

12 pitted black olives, sliced (see Note)

2 eggs

250 ml (8 fl oz/1 cup) milk

3 tablespoons olive oil

1 **Preheat the oven** to 200°C (400°F/Gas 6). Generously grease one 20 x 10 cm (8 x 4 inch) loaf tin.

2 **Squeeze as much** moisture from the zucchini as possible and set aside.

3 **In a large bowl,** sift the flour, baking powder, salt and sugar. Add the cheddar cheese, chives and olives. Beat the eggs and add the milk, oil and the zucchini and combine.

4 **Make a well** in the centre of the dry ingredients and add the zucchini mixture. Stir for 30 seconds, or until well combined.

5 **Pour into the prepared** tin and bake for 35–40 minutes, or until a skewer inserted in the centre comes out clean. Leave to rest for 5 minutes, then turn out onto a wire rack to cool.

Note: The best olives to use are Spanish as Kalamata olives taste a little bitter when cooked.

DRIED TOMATO AND ROSEMARY FOUGASSE

MAKES 8

1½ teaspoons (4½ g) instant dried yeast

a pinch of caster (superfine) sugar

1½ teaspoons sea salt flakes

2½ tablespoons oil from the sun-dried tomatoes, or extra virgin olive oil, plus extra for brushing

2 teaspoons finely chopped rosemary

150 g (5½ oz) sun-dried tomatoes, drained well (oil reserved) and patted dry

450 g (1 lb/3⅔ cups) plain (all-purpose) flour

1 Sprinkle the yeast and sugar over 125 ml (4 fl oz/ ½ cup) warm water in a small bowl. Stir to dissolve the sugar, then leave in a draught-free place for 10 minutes, or until the yeast is foamy.

2 Transfer the mixture to the bowl of an electric mixer. Add another 185 ml (6 fl oz/ ¾ cup) warm water, sea salt and remaining ingredients, then, using a low speed, mix for 7 minutes, or until the dough is smooth and elastic (the dough will be quite soft). Cover the bowl with a damp cloth and leave to rise in a draught-free place for 1 ½ –2 hours, or until the dough has doubled in size.

3 Knock back the dough by punching it gently, then turn out onto a floured work surface and cut into eight even-sized pieces. Using a floured rolling pin, roll out each piece to form an 18 x 9 cm (7 x 3 ½ inch) oval shape. Place the fougasse on a board and, using a sharp knife, cut angled slits down each half of the oval, cutting through to the board (do not cut through the edges of the dough). Gently pull the cuts apart to form long gaps. Transfer to two greased baking trays, brush with olive oil, then cover loosely with a damp cloth. Leave for 20–25 minutes, or until slightly risen and puffy. Meanwhile, preheat the oven to 200°C (400°F/Gas 6).

4 Bake for 20 minutes, or until golden and crisp. Transfer to a wire rack to cool.

GREEK LEMON, DILL AND FETA BREAD

**MAKES TWO 20 X 10 CM
(8 X 4 INCH) LOAVES**

375 g (13 oz/3 cups) white bread
   (strong) flour

125 g (4½ oz/1 cup) semolina

1 tablespoon (12 g) instant dried yeast

1 teaspoon caster (superfine) sugar

2 tablespoons olive oil

60 g (2¼ oz/1 bunch) dill,
   finely chopped

grated zest from 1 lemon

200 g (7 oz/1⅓ cups) coarsely crumbled
   feta cheese, well drained

1   Combine flour, semolina, yeast, sugar and 1½ teaspoons salt in the bowl of an electric mixer with a dough hook attachment. Make a well in the centre. Pour 250 ml (9 fl oz/ 1 cup) warm water and the oil into the well. With mixer set to lowest speed, mix for 3 minutes, or until dough forms. Increase speed to medium, add dill and lemon zest. Knead for another 8 minutes, or until dough is smooth and elastic. Add feta and knead for 2 minutes, or until the feta is incorporated.

2   Alternatively, mix the dough by hand using a wooden spoon, then turn out onto a floured work surface, sprinkle over the dill and lemon zest and knead for 8 minutes or until the dill and zest are incorporated and the dough is smooth and elastic. Pat the dough into a rectangle about 20 x 10 cm (8 x 4 inches) and sprinkle over the feta. Fold the dough over several times, then knead for 2 minutes, or until the feta is incorporated.

3   Grease a large bowl with oil, then transfer the dough to the bowl, turning the dough to coat in the oil. Cover with plastic wrap and leave to rise in a draught-free place for 1½–2 hours, or until the dough has doubled in size.

4   Knock back the dough by punching it gently, then turn out onto a floured work surface. Divide the dough in half and form each into a loaf shape and place, seam side down, into two greased 20 x 10 cm (8 x 4 inch) loaf tins. Cover with a damp cloth and leave for 30 minutes, or until doubled in size. Meanwhile, preheat the oven to 200°C (400°F/Gas 6). Bake the bread for 10 minutes, then reduce the oven to 180°C (350°F/ Gas 4) and bake for a further 20 minutes, or until golden and it sounds hollow when tapped on the base. Transfer to a wire rack to cool.

CARAMELIZED ONION BRAIDS

SERVES 8–10

310 g (10 oz/2½ cups) plain flour
130 g (4¼ oz/1 cup) buckwheat flour
1 teaspoon salt
15 g (½ oz) fresh yeast or 7 g (¼ oz) dried yeast
315 ml (10 fl oz/1¼ cups) warm milk
30 g (1 oz) butter
1 tablespoon oil
1 kg (2 lb) onions, thinly sliced into rings
1 egg, lightly beaten
2 teaspoons fennel seeds

1 Sift the flours and salt into a large bowl and make a well in the centre. Dissolve the yeast in 125 ml (4 fl oz/½ cup) of the warm milk in a small bowl. Then add the remaining warm milk. Pour into the well and mix to a dough. Turn out onto a floured surface and knead for 8 minutes, or until smooth. Place in a large oiled bowl, cover loosely with greased plastic wrap and leave in a warm place for 45 minutes–1 hour, or until doubled in size.

2 Melt the butter and oil in a frying pan, add the onion and cook over a medium-low heat for 40–50 minutes, or until the onion is golden.

3 Punch down the dough, turn out onto a lightly floured surface and knead for about 10 minutes, or until smooth and elastic.

4 Lightly grease two baking trays. Divide the dough in half. Working with 1 piece at a time, divide it into 3 pieces. Roll each piece out to a 30 x 10 cm (12 x 4 inch) rectangle. Divide the onion mixture into six portions and spread a portion along the middle of each rectangle, leaving a 2 cm (¾ inch) border. Brush the edge with some of the beaten egg and roll over lengthways to enclose the filling.

5 Plait the three pieces together and place seam side down on a baking tray. Pinch the ends together.

6 Repeat with the remaining dough and onion. Cover with a damp tea towel and leave in a warm place for about 45 minutes, or until well risen.

7 Preheat the oven to 180°C (350°F/Gas 4). Brush top with beaten egg. Sprinkle with fennel seeds. Bake 35–45 minutes, or until well browned. Transfer to a wire rack to cool.

ONION BUNS

MAKES 12

7 g (¼ oz) dried yeast

1 teaspoon sugar

1 tablespoon olive oil

2 onions, finely chopped

500 g (1 lb/4 cups) plain flour

2 teaspoons salt

1 egg, lightly beaten

1 tablespoon sesame seeds

1   Combine the yeast, sugar and 125 ml (4 fl oz/½ cup) of warm water in a bowl. Cover and set aside in a warm place for 10 minutes, or until frothy.

2   Heat the oil in a frying pan and cook the onion until golden.

3   Sift the flour and salt into a bowl. Stir in the onion and make a well in the centre. Pour in 250 ml (8 fl oz/1 cup) of warm water and the yeast. Mix to a soft dough and knead for 10 minutes, or until smooth. Place in a lightly oiled bowl, cover loosely with greased plastic wrap and leave in a warm place for 1 hour, or until doubled in size.

4   Grease twelve 125 ml (4 fl oz/½ cup) muffin tins.

5   Punch down the dough, turn out onto a lightly floured surface and knead for 1 minute. Divide the dough into 12 portions and shape each portion into a ball. Place in the tin, cover loosely with a damp team towel (dish towel) and set aside in a warm place for 30 minutes, or until well risen.

6   Preheat the oven to 180°C (350°F/Gas 4). Brush buns with egg and sprinkle with sesame seeds. Bake for about 30 minutes, or until crusty.

TAHINI SPIRALS

MAKES 10

1 teaspoon (3 g) instant dried yeast	
1 teaspoon caster (superfine) sugar	
1 tablespoon olive oil	
335 g (12 oz/2⅔ cups) white bread (strong) flour	
90 g (3¼ oz/⅓ cup) tahini	
60 g (2¼ oz/⅓ cup) soft brown sugar	
2 teaspoons vegetable oil	

1 **Sprinkle the yeast** and sugar over 250 ml (9 fl oz/1 cup) warm water in a large bowl. Stir to dissolve the sugar, then leave in a draught-free place for 10 minutes, or until yeast is foamy, then stir in the olive oil.

2 **Combine the yeast mixture** and a third of the flour in the bowl of an electric mixer with a dough hook attachment. With the mixer set to the lowest speed, gradually add the remaining flour, 60 g (2¼ oz/½ cup) at a time, mixing until a dough forms. Increase speed to medium and knead for 7 minutes, or until the dough is smooth and elastic. Alternatively, mix the dough by hand using a wooden spoon, then turn out onto a floured work surface and knead dough for 7 minutes, or until smooth and elastic.

3 **Grease a large bowl** with oil, then transfer the dough to the bowl, turning the dough to coat in the oil. Cover with plastic wrap and leave to rise in a draught-free place for 2 hours, or until the dough has doubled in size.

4 **Preheat the oven** to 190°C (375°F/Gas 5). Lightly grease two baking trays. Put the tahini, brown sugar and vegetable oil in a small bowl, stirring to mix well.

5 **Knock back dough** by punching it gently, then turn out onto a floured work surface and divide into 10 equal portions. Working with one portion at a time, roll out each to form a 20 x 10 cm (8 x 4 inch) rectangle. Spread about 1 tablespoon of tahini mixture over the dough, spreading it to the edges. Starting at the long edge of the rectangle, roll it up to form a long cylinder. Tightly coil the cylinder to form a round, then tuck the end underneath. Transfer spirals to prepared baking trays and, using the palm of your hand, flatten slightly. Bake for 12–15 minutes, or until golden. Serve warm.

HOT CROSS BUNS

MAKES 16

1 tablespoon (12 g) instant dried yeast

80 g (2¾ oz/⅓ cup) caster (superfine) sugar

625 g (1 lb 6 oz/5 cups) white bread (strong) flour

1½ teaspoons mixed (pumpkin pie) spice

1 teaspoon ground cinnamon

1 teaspoon ground nutmeg

250 ml (9 fl oz/1 cup) warm milk

100 g (3½ oz) unsalted butter, melted

2 eggs, lightly beaten

200 g (7 oz/1⅓ cups) currants

70 g (2½ oz/⅓ cup) mixed candied citrus peel

GLAZE

2 tablespoons caster (superfine) sugar

CROSS DOUGH

60 g (2¼ oz/½ cup) plain (all-purpose) flour

1 Sprinkle the yeast and a pinch of the sugar over 125 ml (4 fl oz/½ cup) warm water in a small bowl. Stir to dissolve the sugar, then leave in a draught-free place for 10 minutes, or until the yeast is foamy. Combine the flour, spices and ½ teaspoon salt in a bowl and set aside.

2 Combine the milk, butter, remaining sugar, eggs and 125 g (4½ oz/1 cup) of the flour mixture in the bowl of an electric mixer with a dough hook attachment. Mix 1 minute, or until smooth. Add yeast mixture, currants and mixed peel and stir to combine. Add flour, 125 g (4½ oz/1 cup) at a time, stirring to mix well after each addition. As dough becomes sticky, use lowest speed and knead for 5 minutes.

3 Grease a large bowl with oil, then transfer dough to the bowl, turning the dough to coat it with oil. Cover with plastic wrap and leave to rise for 1 ½–2 hours, until doubled in size.

4 Knock back the dough by punching it gently, then turn out onto a floured work surface. Divide dough into 16 equal portions. Roll each portion into a ball, then place on greased baking trays, spacing the rolls about 4 cm (1 ½ inches) apart. Cover with a damp cloth and leave for 30 minutes, or until doubled in size. Preheat the oven to 180°C (350°F/Gas 4). For the glaze, combine sugar with 2 tablespoons water in a small saucepan. Bring slowly to the boil over high heat,. Remove from the heat and set aside.

5 For the cross dough, put the flour in a small bowl and gradually add 60 ml (2 fl oz/ ¼ cup) water, stirring to form a dough. Roll out dough on a floured surface to a 2 mm (¹/₁₆ inch) thickness. Cut into 5 mm (¼ inch) wide strips, about 12 cm (4½ inches) long. Brush strips with water and place over each bun to form a cross. Bake buns for 15–20 minutes, until golden brown. Glaze the hot buns and cool on a wire rack.

SOUR CREAM POLENTA BREAD

225 g (7 oz/1½ cups) fine polenta
 (see Note)

60 g (2 oz/½ cups) plain flour

2 tablespoons soft brown sugar

1 teaspoon baking powder

½ teaspoon bicarbonate of soda

½ teaspoon salt

1 egg

80 ml (2¾ fl oz/⅓ cup) milk

310 g (10 oz/1¼ cups) sour cream

2 tablespoons vegetable oil

½ teaspoon poppy seeds

1 **Preheat the oven** to 200°C (400°F/Gas 6) and grease one 11 x 18 cm (4½ x 7 inch) loaf tin.

2 **Combine the polenta,** flour, sugar, baking powder, bicarbonate of soda and salt in a large bowl.

3 **Whisk together the egg,** milk, sour cream and oil and add them to the dry ingredients, mixing just long enough for them to be evenly combined. Pour the mixture into the tin and sprinkle with the poppy seeds.

4 **Bake for 30 minutes,** reduce the temperature to 180°C (350°F/Gas 4) and continue baking for a further 15–20 minutes, or until the loaf is golden.

5 **Serve warm,** spread with plenty of butter.

Note: There are different grades of polenta, some being finer than others. Compare different brands before buying. The fine-textured polenta is best for this recipe as it produces a less coarse bread.

SWEET YOGHURT PLAIT

MAKES 2 LOAVES

650 g (1 lb 7 oz/5¼ cups) white bread (strong) flour

1 tablespoon ground cinnamon

3 teaspoons (9 g) instant dried yeast

2 eggs, lightly beaten

250 g (9 oz/1 cup) Greek-style yoghurt

125 ml (4 fl oz/½ cup) lukewarm milk

90 g (3¼ oz/¼ cup) honey

60 g (2¼ oz) butter, chopped

100 g (3½ oz/½ cup) chopped dried figs

GLAZE

1 egg

2 tablespoons milk

ICING

375 g (13 oz/3 cups) icing (confectioners') sugar, sifted

80 ml (2½ fl oz/⅓ cup) lemon juice

1   Combine 600 g (1 lb 5 oz/4¾ cups) of the flour, cinnamon, yeast and 1 teaspoon salt in the bowl of an electric mixer with a dough hook attachment and make a well in the centre. Combine the eggs, yoghurt, milk and honey in a bowl, then pour into the well. With the mixer set to the lowest speed, mix for 3 minutes to combine well. Increase speed to medium and add butter and figs. Knead for 10 minutes, or until the dough is smooth and elastic, adding the remaining flour if the mixture is still sticky. Alternatively, mix dough by hand, using a wooden spoon, then turn out onto a lightly floured work surface and knead for 10 minutes, or until smooth and elastic.

2   Grease a large bowl with oil, then transfer the dough to the bowl, turning the dough to coat in the oil. Cover with plastic wrap and leave to rise in a draught-free place for about 1½ hours, or until the dough has doubled in size.

3   Knock back dough by punching it gently, then turn out onto a floured surface. Cut into six equal portions. Roll each into 30 cm (12 inch) lengths. Plait three lengths, tucking the ends underneath for a neat finish. Repeat for a second loaf.

4   Transfer to a large, lightly greased baking tray. Cover the tray with a damp cloth until the dough has doubled in size (30 minutes) Meanwhile, preheat the oven to 220°C (425° F/Gas 7).

5   To make the glaze, combine the egg and milk and brush over the tops of the loaves. Bake for 10 minutes, then reduce oven to 180°C (350°F/Gas 4) and bake for a further 20 minutes. If the loaves start to brown too quickly, cover them with foil. Transfer to a wire rack to cool.

6   To make the icing, combine icing sugar, lemon juice and 2 tablespoons boiling water in a bowl. Stir until smooth. Drizzle over the cooled loaves. Set aside until the icing has set.

ORANGE AND BLUEBERRY ROLLS

MAKES 20

1 tablespoon (12 g) instant dried yeast

75 g (2½ oz/⅓ cup) caster
(superfine) sugar

250 ml (9 fl oz/1 cup) warm milk

125 g (4½ oz) unsalted butter, softened

80 ml (2½ fl oz/⅓ cup) freshly
squeezed orange juice

2 eggs, lightly beaten

375 g (13 oz/3 cups) white bread
(strong) flour

icing (confectioners') sugar, for dusting

FILLING

100 g (3½ oz) unsalted butter, softened

115 g (4 oz/½ cup) caster
(superfine) sugar

grated zest from 2 oranges

270 g (9½ oz/1¾ cups) blueberries

1 **Sprinkle yeast** and a pinch of sugar over 100 ml (3 ½ fl oz) warm milk in a small bowl. Stir to dissolve sugar, then leave in a draught-free place for 10 minutes, or until the yeast is foamy.

2 **Put the remaining milk** and sugar, the butter and 1 teaspoon salt in the bowl of an electric mixer. Using the beater attachment, mix until the butter has just melded in. Add the orange juice, eggs and yeast mixture and mix to combine. Using the lowest speed, gradually add the flour, 60 g (2 ¼ oz/ ½ cup) at a time, mixing until the dough is soft and smooth.

3 **Grease a large bowl** with oil. Transfer dough to the bowl, turning it to coat in the oil. Cover with plastic wrap and leave to rise in a draught-free place for 1 hour, or until the dough has doubled in size.

4 **To make the filling,** cream the butter, sugar and orange zest in a small bowl using electric beaters until pale and fluffy.

5 **Grease two 20 cm** (8 inch) round spring-form cake tins.

6 **Turn dough out** onto a lightly floured work surface and divide in half. Roll each piece into a 25 x 15 cm (10 x 6 inch) rectangle. Spread half the filling mixture over one rectangle, then arrange half the blueberries over the top. Repeat with the remaining rectangle of dough, filling and blueberries. Starting from the long side, roll up each rectangle to form a cylinder. Then, using a lightly floured, serrated knife, cut each cylinder into 10 equal rolls. Arrange 10 rolls, cut side up, over the base of each tin. Cover with a damp cloth and leave for 45 minutes, or until the rolls have doubled in size.

7 **Meanwhile,** preheat the oven to 180°C (350°F/Gas 4). Bake rolls for 25–30 minutes, or until golden and they come away from the sides of the tins. Cool in tins for 5 minutes, then transfer to a wire rack to cool. Dust with icing sugar to serve.

FINNISH CARDAMOM RINGS

MAKES 16

1 tablespoon (12 g) instant dried yeast

115 g (4 oz/½ cup) caster (superfine) sugar

200 ml (7 fl oz) evaporated milk

2 eggs, lightly beaten

80 g (2¾ oz/½ cup) wholemeal (whole-wheat) flour

500 g (1 lb 2 oz/4 cups) white bread (strong) flour

1½ teaspoons ground cardamom

50 g (1¾ oz) unsalted butter, softened

GLAZE

1 egg

60 ml (2 fl oz/¼ cup) milk

1 **Sprinkle yeast** and 1 teaspoon of the sugar over 125 ml (4 fl oz/½ cup) warm water in a small bowl. Stir to dissolve the sugar, then leave in a draught-free place for 10 minutes, or until the yeast is foamy.

2 **Combine** the evaporated milk and eggs in a small bowl and stir to mix well.

3 **Combine wholemeal flour,** 250 g (9 oz/2 cups) of white bread flour, the cardamom, remaining sugar and 1½ teaspoons salt in the bowl of an electric mixer with a dough hook and make a well in the centre. Pour in the yeast and evaporated milk mixtures. With the mixer set to the lowest speed, mix for 1 minute, or until a dough forms. Add the butter and mix to combine well. Add the remaining flour, 60 g (2¼ oz/½ cup) at a time, and knead for 10 minutes, or until the dough is smooth and elastic (the dough will be very soft).

4 **Grease a large bowl** with oil, then transfer the dough to the bowl, turning the dough to coat in the oil. Cover with plastic wrap and leave to rise in a draught-free place for 1–1½ hours, or until the dough has doubled in size.

5 **Knock back the dough** by punching it gently, then turn out onto a floured surface. Divide dough into 16 equal portions. Using your hands, roll each piece of dough to measure 25 cm (10 inches) in length, then join the ends to form a ring. Gently press the joins to seal. Transfer rings to two lightly greased baking trays. Cover loosely with a damp cloth and leave for 45 minutes, or until doubled in size. Meanwhile, preheat the oven to 180°C (350°F/Gas 4).

6 **To make glaze,** whisk together the egg and milk and brush it over rings. Bake for 18–20 minutes, or until golden.

ITALIAN DRIED FRUIT BUNS

MAKES 12

90 g (3¼ oz/¾ cup) raisins

3 teaspoons (9 g) instant dried yeast

80 g (2¾ oz/⅓ cup) caster (superfine) sugar

400 g (14 oz/3¼ cups) white bread (strong) flour

1 teaspoon almond essence

1 tablespoon olive oil

finely grated zest from 1 orange

40 g (1½ oz/¼ cup) mixed candied citrus peel

40 g (1½ oz/¼ cup) pine nuts

1 egg, lightly beaten

115 g (4 oz/½ cup) caster (superfine) sugar, extra

1 Cover the raisins with 250 ml (9 fl oz/1 cup) boiling water in a small bowl and set aside for 20 minutes. Drain, reserving liquid. Put half the liquid into a bowl, add the yeast, a pinch of the sugar and 30 g (1 oz/¼ cup) of flour. Stir to combine. Leave in a draught-free place for 10 minutes, or until yeast is foamy.

2 Sift remaining flour, sugar and 1 teaspoon salt into the bowl of an electric mixer with a dough hook attachment and make a well in the centre. Combine the remaining raisin water with the almond essence and oil, then pour it, along with the yeast mixture, into the well. Add raisins, orange zest, mixed peel and pine nuts. With mixer set to the lowest speed, mix until a dough forms. Increase speed to medium and knead dough for 5 minutes, or until it is smooth and elastic; add a little more flour, if necessary. Alternatively, mix dough by hand using a wooden spoon, then turn out onto a floured work surface and knead for 5 minutes, or until smooth and elastic.

3 Grease a large bowl with oil, then transfer the dough to the bowl, turning the dough to coat in the oil. Cover with plastic wrap and leave to rise in a draught-free place for 2 hours, or until the dough has doubled in size.

4 Knock back the dough by punching it gently, then turn out onto a lightly floured work surface. Divide the dough into 12 equal portions and shape each piece into an oval. To glaze the rolls, coat them in egg, then roll them in the extra sugar to coat. Transfer the rolls to a greased baking tray and leave for 30–40 minutes, or until the rolls have risen a little (they won't quite double in size). Meanwhile, preheat the oven to 200°C (400°F/Gas 6).

5 Bake the rolls for 15 minutes, or until golden, then transfer to a wire rack to cool.

SAFFRON CURRANT BREAD

MAKES ONE 25 CM (10 INCH) RING

110 g (3¾ oz/¾ cup) currants

2 tablespoons dry sherry or rum

60 ml (2 fl oz/¼ cup) milk

¼ teaspoon saffron threads

1 tablespoon (12 g) instant dried yeast

115 g (4 oz/½ cup) caster (superfine) sugar

125 g (4½ oz) unsalted butter, softened

3 eggs

25 g (1 oz/¼ cup) ground almonds

grated zest from 1 orange

375 g (13 oz/3 cups) plain (all-purpose) flour

icing (confectioners') sugar, for dusting

1   Combine the currants and sherry in a small bowl and set aside for 30 minutes. Heat milk in a small saucepan over medium heat until it reaches simmering point, then remove from the heat. Add the saffron and set aside for 20 minutes to allow the saffron to infuse.

2   Sprinkle the yeast and a pinch of the sugar over 60 ml (2 fl oz/¼ cup) warm water in a small bowl. Stir to dissolve sugar, then leave in a draught-free place for 10 minutes, or until the yeast is foamy. Grease a 25 cm (10 inch) ring tin.

3   Cream the butter and remaining sugar in a bowl using an electric mixer until pale and fluffy. Add the eggs one at a time, beating well after each addition. Add ½ teaspoon salt, the milk and yeast mixtures, ground almonds, orange zest and currant

mixture and beat gently to combine. Add the flour, 60 g (2¼ oz/½ cup) at a time, and mix until incorporated. Using the lowest speed, beat the mixture for another 5 minutes, or until the dough is shiny and elastic (the dough will be soft).

4   Spoon dough into the prepared ring tin. Cover with plastic wrap. Leave to rise in a draught-free place for 1½–2 hours, or until the dough has doubled in size. Meanwhile, preheat the oven to 180°C (350°F/Gas 4).

5   Bake the bread for 35–40 minutes, or until golden, and a skewer inserted in the centre of the bread comes out clean. Cool in the tin for 10 minutes, then turn out onto a wire rack to cool. Serve dusted with icing sugar.

CHOCOLATE BREAD

MAKES TWO 20 CM (8 INCH) LOAVES

2½ teaspoons (7 g) instant dried yeast

55 g (2 oz/¼ cup) caster (superfine) sugar

90 g (3¼ oz/⅔ cup) dark chocolate, roughly chopped

50 g (1¾ oz) unsalted butter

375 g (13 oz/3 cups) white bread (strong) flour

30 g (1 oz/¼ cup) unsweetened cocoa powder

1 egg, lightly beaten

½ teaspoon natural vanilla extract

90 g (3¼ oz/½ cup) dark chocolate chips

1 **Sprinkle yeast** and a pinch of the sugar over 185 ml 6 fl oz/¾ cup) warm water in a small bowl. Stir to dissolve the sugar. Leave in a draught-free place for 10 minutes, until yeast foams.

2 **Put the chocolate** and butter in a heatproof bowl. Sit the bowl over a saucepan of simmering water, stirring frequently until chocolate and butter have melted. Take care that the base of the bowl doesn't touch the water.

3 **Combine flour,** cocoa powder, ¼ teaspoon salt and the remaining sugar in the bowl of an electric mixer with a dough hook attachment. Combine egg and vanilla with chocolate and butter. Pour chocolate and yeast mixtures into the flour mixture. With mixer set to the lowest speed, mix for 1–2 minutes, or until a dough forms. Increase speed to medium and knead the dough for another 10 minutes, or until dough is smooth and elastic. Alternatively, mix the dough by hand using a wooden spoon, then turn out onto a floured work surface and knead for 10 minutes, or until the dough is smooth and elastic.

4 **Grease a large bowl** with oil. Transfer dough to the bowl, turning it to coat in the oil. Cover with plastic wrap and leave to rise in a draught-free place for 1½–2 hours, or until the dough has doubled in size.

5 **Knock back dough** by punching it gently, then turn out onto a floured work surface. Divide dough in half. Gently press out each half until 1 cm (½ inch) thick, then scatter chocolate chips over each. Roll up each piece of dough to form a log. Place on a greased baking tray. Cover with a damp cloth and leave for 1 hour, or until doubled in size. Meanwhile, preheat the oven to 180°C (350°F/Gas 4). Bake 45–50 minutes, until bread is light brown and sounds hollow when tapped on the base. Cool on a wire rack.

PLUM AND ROSEMARY FLATBREAD

MAKES ONE 25 CM (10 INCH) ROUND BREAD

60 ml (2 fl oz/¼ cup) warm milk

2 teaspoons (6 g) instant dried yeast

115 g (4 oz/½ cup) caster (superfine) sugar

2 eggs, lightly beaten

grated zest from 1 lemon

2 teaspoons finely chopped rosemary

185 g (6½ oz/1½ cups) white bread (strong) flour

150 g (5½ oz) unsalted butter, softened, cut into pieces

10 plums, halved and stoned, or 800 g (1 lb 12 oz) tinned plums, drained

whipped cream or mascarpone, to serve

1 **Grease** a 25 cm (10 inch) spring-form cake tin or a loose-based flan tin with butter.

2 **Combine the milk and yeast** in the bowl of an electric mixer. Stir in 55 g (2 oz/¼ cup) of the sugar, eggs, lemon zest and 1 teaspoon of the rosemary, then add the flour. Using the beater attachment, mix for 1 minute, or until a soft dough forms. Add the butter, then continue mixing for a further minute, or until the dough is smooth, shiny and thick. Alternatively, mix the dough by hand using a wooden spoon.

3 **Spoon into the prepared tin.** Cover with plastic wrap. Leave in a draught-free place for 1½–2 hours, or until dough has doubled in size.

4 **Knock back dough** by punching it gently. Dampen the palms of your hands with water and press dough into the edges of the tin. Arrange the plums, cut side up, over the top, pressing them gently into the dough. Leave for 30 minutes. Meanwhile, preheat the oven to 200°C (400°F/Gas 6).

5 **Sprinkle plums** with the remaining sugar and scatter over the remaining rosemary. Bake for 10 minutes, then reduce the oven to 180°C (350°F/Gas 4) and bake for 20 minutes, or until light golden and slightly spongy when pressed in the centre. Serve warm, cut into wedges, with cream or mascarpone.

FRUIT AND TEA LOAF

**MAKES ONE 25 X 11 CM
(10 X 4¼ INCH) LOAF**

500 g (1 lb 2 oz/2¾ cups) mixed
  dried fruit

185 ml (6 fl oz/¾ cup) strong, hot
  black tea

125 g (4½ oz/⅔ cup) lightly packed soft
  brown sugar

1 egg, lightly beaten

125 g (4½ oz/1 cup) plain
  (all-purpose) flour

¾ teaspoon baking powder

1 teaspoon ground cinnamon

¼ teaspoon ground nutmeg

a large pinch of ground cloves

1   Combine the fruit and hot tea in a large bowl, cover with plastic wrap and leaver for 3 hours or overnight.

2   Preheat the oven to 160°C (315°F/Gas 2–3). Grease a 25 x 11 cm (10 x 4¼ inch) loaf tin and line the base with baking paper. Dust the sides of the tin with a little flour, shaking off any excess.

3   Stir the sugar and egg into the fruit mixture to combine well. Sift flour, baking powder and spices into a bowl, then add fruit mixture. Using a large slotted spoon, stir to combine well.

4   Spoon the mixture into the tin and bake for 1 hour 35 minutes. Cover the top with foil if it browns too quickly. The loaf is cooked when a skewer inserted in the centre of the loaf comes out clean. Cool the loaf in the tin. This loaf is good spread with butter.

5   The loaf will keep, wrapped in plastic wrap and stored in an airtight container in a cool place, for up to 1 week, or up to 8 weeks in the freezer.

PASTRY

PASTRY BASICS

SHORTCRUST PASTRY
Makes 380 g (13½ oz)

200 g (7 oz/1⅔ cups) plain (all-purpose) flour, sifted

120 g (4¼ oz) chilled unsalted butter, chopped

1 **If making pastry using a food processor,** put the flour, butter and ¼ teaspoon salt in the food processor. Using the pulse button, process until the mixture resembles coarse breadcrumbs. Add 60 ml (2 fl oz/¼ cup) chilled water, adding the water gradually, and pulse just until a dough forms, being careful not to overprocess. If the dough is dry and not coming together, add a little more water, 1 teaspoon at a time. As soon as the mixture comes together, turn it out onto a lightly floured work surface and press into a flat disc. Cover with plastic wrap and refrigerate for 30 minutes.

2 **If making the pastry by hand,** sift flour and salt into a large bowl. Add the butter. Using your fingertips, rub the butter into the flour until the mixture resembles coarse breadcrumbs. Make a well in the centre. Pour 60 ml (2 fl oz/ ¼ cup) chilled water into the well, then stir with a flat-bladed knife to incorporate the water. When the mixture starts to come together in small beads of dough, gently gather it together and lift it out onto a lightly floured work surface. Gently press the dough together into a ball, kneading it lightly if necessary until the dough comes together. Press into a flat disc, cover with plastic wrap and refrigerate for 30 minutes. The dough is now ready to use. Roll out the dough and proceed as directed in the recipe.

SWEET SHORTCRUST PASTRY
Makes 400 g (14 oz)

200 g (7 oz/1⅔ cups) plain (all-purpose) flour, sifted

85 g (3 oz/⅔ cup) icing (confectioners') sugar, sifted

100 g (3½ oz) chilled unsalted butter, chopped

1 egg yolk

1 **If making pastry using a food processor,** put the flour, icing sugar, butter and a pinch of salt in the food processor. Using the pulse button, process until the mixture resembles coarse breadcrumbs. Combine the egg yolk with 1 tablespoon chilled water in a small bowl. Add to the flour mixture and, using the pulse button, process until a dough forms, being careful not to overprocess. If the dough is dry and not coming together, add a little more water, 1 teaspoon at a time. Turn out onto a lightly floured work surface and press the dough into a flat, round disc. Cover with plastic wrap and refrigerate for 30 minutes.

2 **If making the pastry by hand,** sift the flour, icing sugar and a pinch of salt into a large bowl, then add the butter. Using your fingertips, rub the butter into the flour until the mixture resembles coarse breadcrumbs. Make a well in the centre. Combine the egg yolk with 1 tablespoon chilled water in a small bowl. Pour it into the well, then stir with a flat-bladed knife. When the mixture starts to come together in small beads of dough, gently gather the dough together and lift it out onto a lightly floured work surface. Gently press the dough together into a ball, then press into a flat disc. Cover with plastic wrap and refrigerate for 30 minutes. The dough is now ready to use. Roll out the dough and proceed as directed in the recipe.

Notes: The kitchen needs to be as cool as possible when making pastry. It is really important not to overwork the dough or it will become tough. Butter should be cold, straight from the refrigerator. Cut the butter into even sized pieces, about 5 mm (¼ inch) thick. Always used chilled water to bind the dough. Flour should be sifted before use. This will remove any lumps and incorporate air into the flour, helping to make the dough light. Always rest dough in the refrigerator for at least 30 minutes. If the dough is too cold to roll out it will crack easily, so leave at room temperature, still covered in plastic wrap, for 15 minutes to soften. Always roll from the middle outwards (not using a back-and-forth motion) and rotate the pastry frequently as you go to keep the required shape. If the dough feels really soft and starts to stick to the work surface, roll it out between two sheets of baking paper. Shortcrust (and sweet shortcrust) pastry keeps well once made. Cover with plastic wrap and refrigerate for up to 3 days. It also freezes for up to 3 months.

1 Preheat the oven to 200°C (400°F/Gas 6). Lightly grease or line a baking tray with baking paper. Put the water, butter and sugar in a small saucepan and heat until the butter has melted and the mixture has just come to the boil. Add the flour and, using a wooden spoon, stir over medium heat until the mixture comes away from the side of the saucepan, forming a ball. Place the mixture in the bowl of an electric mixer fitted with a whisk attachment and allow to cool slightly. Add the eggs one at a time, beating energetically after each addition and making sure that each egg is thoroughly incorporated before adding the next. (Alternatively, you use a hand mixer or wooden spoon to mix the ingredients.) The mixture should be thick and glossy. The pastry is now ready to use. Pipe, spoon or shape it according to the recipe you are using.

2 To make choux puffs, place teaspoonfuls of the mixture on lightly oiled baking trays, spacing them 4 cm (1½ inches) apart. Bake for 25 minutes, or until puffed and golden. Turn off the oven. Using a skewer or small, sharp knife, pierce the base or top of each profiterole to release the steam (they will turn soggy, if you don't). Return the profiteroles to the oven, leave the door slightly open, and let them dry out for about 15 minutes. Transfer to a wire rack to cool completely.

3 To make eclairs, put the choux pastry into a piping bag fitted with a 2 cm (¾ inch) plain nozzle. Pipe 10 cm (4 inch) lengths of choux onto the baking tray, spacing them 4 cm (1½ inches) apart. Bake as for choux puffs.

For the best results: Always preheat the oven before beginning to make the choux pastry because it is cooked immediately after it is shaped or piped. Add the flour to the boiling mixture in one go. Immediately beat the mixture with a wooden spoon to prevent lumps forming. Stop beating as soon as the soft dough comes away from the side of the pan and remove from the heat. Always allow the hot mixture to cool for 2–3 minutes before adding eggs or they will start to cook. Beat in the eggs one at a time, making sure they are completely incorporated before adding the next egg. Vigorous action is required. The dough should be piped or shaped while it is still warm. Leave 4 cm (1½ inches) between the piped or spooned dough, allowing room for spreading during cooking. Choux pastries will keep, stored in an airtight container, for up to 3 days. To refresh, if necessary, place on a baking tray and heat in a preheated 180°C (350°F/Gas 4) oven for about 8 minutes, or until the pastry is dry and crisp.

CHOUX PASTRY

Makes about 40 choux puffs and
  16 eclairs

250 ml (9 fl oz/1 cup) water
100 g (3½ oz) unsalted butter
1 teaspoon caster (superfine) sugar
140 g (5 oz) plain (all-purpose) flour
3 eggs

Lining a tart tin

Carefully fold the pastry back over and around the rolling pin and lift it gently from the work surface.

Unroll over the tin and ease in, pressing to fit the sides. Roll the pin across the top to cut off the excess dough.

Baking blind

Line the tin with baking paper, then pour in baking beads, uncooked rice or dried pulses (eg, chickpeas, lentils).

Cook for 15 minutes at 200°C (400°F). Lift out paper and beads and bake for a further 5 minutes..

POPPY SEED AND PARMESAN FILO ROLLS

MAKES 30

125 g (4½ oz/1¼ cups) grated parmesan cheese

35 g (1¼ oz/⅓ cup) dry breadcrumbs

2½ tablespoons poppy seeds

2 egg yolks, lightly beaten

5 sheets filo pastry

80 g (2¾ oz) butter, melted

1 **Preheat the oven** to 180°C (350°F/Gas 4). Lightly grease a baking tray.

2 **Combine the parmesan,** breadcrumbs and poppy seeds in a bowl and season with freshly ground black pepper. Add the egg yolks, then, using a fork, work the yolks into the parmesan mixture until the mixture begins to clump together.

3 **Place a sheet of filo pastry** on the work surface, leaving the remaining sheets under a dampened tea towel (dish towel). Brush the pastry with some of the butter, then fold in half lengthways. Brush the pastry with the butter again, then sprinkle evenly with 45 g (1½ oz/⅓ cup slightly heaped) of parmesan mixture. Roll up the pastry as tightly as possible to form a long, thin log. Cut the log evenly into six rolls, then place the rolls, seam side down, on the baking tray. Repeat with the remaining pastry and filling mixture.

4 **Brush rolls** with melted butter, then bake for 20 minutes, or until golden and crisp. Cool slightly, then serve warm or at room temperature, with drinks.

PRAWN, CRAB AND CHEESE MINI QUICHES

MAKES 4

2 cups (250 g/8 oz) plain flour

125 g (4 oz) cold butter, chopped

2 egg yolks

CRAB AND CHEESE FILLING

170 g (5½ oz) can crabmeat, drained
   and squeezed dry

4 spring onions, chopped

2 eggs, lightly beaten

1 cup (250 ml/8 fl oz) cream

1 cup (125 g/4 oz) finely grated cheddar
   cheese

2 tablespoons chopped dill

1 teaspoon grated lemon rind

200 g (6½ oz) small prawns (shrimp),
   cooked and peeled

1 **Process the flour** and butter for 15 seconds, or until crumbly. Add the egg yolks and 3–4 tablespoons of water. Process in short bursts until the mixture comes together. Add a little extra water, if needed.

2 **Turn out onto a floured** surface and gather into a ball. Cover the pastry with plastic wrap and refrigerate for at least 15 minutes.

3 **Grease eight 3 cm** (1¼ inch) deep loose-based flan tins, measuring 8 cm (3 inches) across the base.

4 **Divide pastry** into 8 equal pieces and roll out so they are large enough to fit and overlap the tins. Fit the pastry into the tins and trim off any excess using a sharp knife. Cover and refrigerate for 15 minutes.

5 **Preheat the oven** to 190°C (375°F/Gas 5). Cover pastry shells with baking paper and fill evenly with baking beads. Bake for 10 minutes. Remove the paper and beads and bake for a further 10 minutes.

6 **To make the filling,** place crabmeat, spring onions, beaten eggs, cream, cheese, chopped dill and lemon rind in a bowl. Season with freshly ground black pepper. Divide the prawns between the pastry shells. The crab mixture will be quite thick, so use a fork to help spread it over the prawns.

7 **Bake quiches** for 15–20 minutes, or until the filling is golden brown.

SWEET POTATO AND LENTIL POUCHES

MAKES 32

2 tablespoons olive oil

1 large leek, white part only, finely
  chopped

2 garlic cloves, crushed

125 g (4½ oz/1⅓ cups) chopped button
  mushrooms

2 teaspoons ground cumin

2 teaspoons ground coriander

95 g (3¼ oz/½ cup) brown or green
  lentils

125 g (4½ oz/½ cup) red lentils

500 ml (17 fl oz/2 cups) vegetable stock

300 g (10½ oz) sweet potato, peeled
  and diced

4 tablespoons chopped coriander
  (cilantro)

8 sheets of frozen puff pastry, thawed

1 egg, lightly beaten

YOGHURT SAUCE

200 g (7 oz) plain yoghurt

2 tablespoons grated Lebanese (short)
  cucumber

½ teaspoon soft brown sugar

1 Heat the olive oil in a saucepan. Sauté the leek over medium heat for 3 minutes. Add the garlic, mushroom and ground spices and cook for 1 minute, or until fragrant.

2 Add the lentils and stock and bring to the boil. Reduce the heat and simmer for 20–25 minutes, or until the lentils are tender, stirring occasionally. Add the sweet potato during the last 5 minutes. Stir in the coriander, season to taste and leave to cool.

3 Meanwhile, preheat the oven to 200°C (400°F/Gas 6). Cut each sheet of pastry into four squares. Place 1½ tablespoons of filling into the centre of each and bring the edges together to form a pouch. Pinch together, then tie each pouch with string. Lightly brush with egg and place on lined baking trays.

4 Bake for 20–25 minutes, or until puffed and golden. Remove the strings.

5 Put the yoghurt, cucumber and sugar in a bowl and mix to make a sauce. Serve with the hot pouches.

FETA AND PINE NUT STRUDEL

SERVES 4–6

½ cup (80 g/2¾ oz) pine nuts, toasted

1¾ cups (260 g/8 oz) feta cheese, crumbled

250 g (8 oz) ricotta cheese

2 tablespoons chopped basil

4 spring onions, chopped

2 eggs, lightly beaten

9 sheets filo pastry

40 g (1¼ oz) butter

2 tablespoons olive oil

2–3 teaspoons sesame seeds

1 **Preheat the oven** to 180°C (350°F/Gas 4).

2 **Combine the pine nuts,** feta, ricotta, basil, spring onion and eggs. Season with freshly ground black pepper.

3 **Brush each sheet of filo** with the combined melted butter and oil and stack them one on top of the other.

4 **Spread the cheese filling** in the centre, covering an area of about 10 x 30 cm (4 x 12 inches). Fold in the sides of the pastry, then tuck in the ends. Carefully turn the strudel over and place on a baking tray, seam-side-down. Lightly brush the top with a little melted butter and sprinkle with the sesame seeds.

5 **Bake for 35 minutes,** or until the pastry is crisp and golden. Serve warm with relish or chutney.

POTATO, FETA AND ROAST GARLIC PASTIES

SERVES 8–10

300 g (10½ oz) all-purpose potatoes
   (such as pontiacs), unpeeled

8 garlic cloves

2 teaspoons rosemary leaves, chopped

2 tablespoons extra virgin olive oil

80 g (2¾ oz) feta cheese, crumbled

½ teaspoon grated lemon zest

sea salt

2 quantities shortcrust pastry
   (see page 36)

1 egg yolk

1 tablespoon milk

1 Preheat the oven to 180°C (350°F/Gas 4). Lightly grease a baking tray.

2 Boil the potatoes in their skins for 15 minutes, or until just cooked. Drain, allow to cool, then peel and cut into 1 cm (½ inch) pieces.

3 Put the garlic, rosemary and 1 tablespoon of the oil onto a piece of foil, then twist the edges together to make a secure package. Place on the baking tray and roast for 30 minutes. Allow to cool, then squeeze the garlic from its skin and roughly chop.

4 Add the garlic to the potato, along with the rosemary and any oil left in the foil package. Add the remaining oil, the feta and lemon zest. Gently toss together to combine well. Season well with freshly ground black pepper and a little sea salt.

5 Divide the pastry in half. Roll out each half to a 3 mm (⅛ inch) thickness, then cut into a total of eight 15 cm (6 inch) rounds. Put 2 tablespoons of filling on one half of a pastry round. Combine the egg yolk and milk in a small bowl and lightly brush the unfilled half of the pastry with the egg mix. Fold over the pastry to enclose the filling, pressing gently to seal well. Crimp the edge with your fingers, or gently press with the tines of a fork. Repeat with the remaining filling and pastry rounds.

6 Place the pasties onto the tray, brush the tops with the remaining egg mix, then put the tray in the refrigerator for at least 30 minutes. Remove and bake for 30 minutes, or until golden. Allow the pasties to cool a little before serving, as the filling will be steaming hot.

CHICKEN AND CORN PIES

MAKES 6

1 tablespoon olive oil

650 g (1 lb 7 oz) chicken thigh fillets, trimmed and cut into 1 cm (½ inch) pieces

1 tablespoon grated ginger

400 g (14 oz) oyster mushrooms, halved

3 corn cobs, kernels removed

125 ml (4 fl oz/½ cup) chicken stock

2 tablespoons kecap manis

2 tablespoons cornflour (cornstarch)

30 g (1 oz/1 cup) coriander (cilantro) leaves, chopped

6 sheets ready-rolled shortcrust pastry

milk, to glaze

1   Grease six metal pie tins measuring 9.5 cm (3¾ inches) on the base and 3 cm (1¼ inches) deep. Heat the oil in a large frying pan over high heat and add the chicken. Cook for 5 minutes, or until golden: Add the ginger, mushrooms' and corn and cook for 5-6 minutes, or until the chicken is just cooked through. Add the stock and kecap manis.

2   Mix the cornflour with 2 tablespoons water in a small bowl or jug, then stir into the pan. Boil for 2 minutes before adding the coriander. Transfer to a bowl, cool a little, then refrigerate for 2 hours, or until cold.

3   Preheat the oven to moderate 180°C (350°F/Gas 4).

4   Using a saucer to guide you, cut a 15 cm (6 inch) round from each sheet of shortcrust pastry and line the six pie tins. Fill the shells with the cooled filling, then cut out another six rounds large enough to make the lids. Top the pies with the lids, cut away any extra pastry and seal the edges with a fork. Decorate the pies with shapes cut from pastry scraps. Prick a few holes in the top of each pie, brush with a little milk and bake for 35 minutes, or until golden.

STEAK AND KIDNEY PIE

SERVES 6

60 g (2 oz/1½ cups) plain (all-purpose)
flour seasoned

1.5 kg (3 lb 5 oz) chuck steak, cut into
2 cm (¾ inch) cubes

1 ox kidney (500 g/1 lb 2 oz), cut into
2 cm (¾ inch) cubes

2 tablespoons olive oil

2 onions, chopped

125 g (4½ oz) button mushrooms
quartered

40 g (1½ oz) butter

250 ml (8 fl oz/1 cup) beef or veal stock

185 ml (6 fl oz/¾ cup) stout

2 tablespoons worcestershire sauce

1 tablespoon anchovy essence

1 tablespoon chopped flat-leaf (Italian)
parsley

600 g (1 lb 5 oz) puff pastry

1 egg, lightly beaten

1 **Place the flour in a bowl.** Toss the steak and kidney pieces through the flour and shake off any excess.

2 **Heat the oil** in a large pan over a medium heat, add the onion and cook for 5 minutes. Add the mushrooms and cook for 5 minutes. Remove from the pan.

3 **Melt a third** of the butter in the pan, add a third of the beef and kidney and cook over medium heat, turning occasionally, for 5 minutes, or until brown. Remove and repeat twice with the remaining butter, beef and kidney. Return all the meat to the pan. Add the stock and the stout. Stir and bring slowly to the boil. Reduce heat and simmer for 2 hours. Remove from heat. Leave to cool, then add onion and mushrooms, worcestershire sauce, anchovy essence and parsley.

4 **Preheat the oven** to 180°C (350°F/Gas 4). Place filling in a ceramic pie dish 20 cm (8 inches) across the base and 4 cm (1½ inches) deep. Roll out the pastry between two sheets of baking paper to fit the top of the pie dish. Moisten the rim of the dish with milk and place the pastry over the filling. Press firmly into place and brush with egg. Decorate with pastry scraps, brush with egg.

5 **Bake for 40–45 minutes** until pastry is golden.

TOMATO, GOAT'S CHEESE AND CARAMELIZED ONION FLAN

1 quantity shortcrust pastry (page 36)
2 tablespoons olive oil
3 onions, peeled and thinly sliced
60 g (2¼ oz) goat's cheese
3 roma (plum) tomatoes, cut into 5 mm (¼ inch) thick slices
½ teaspoon thyme
6 egg yolks
2 eggs, lightly beaten
250 ml (9 fl oz/1 cup) cream

1 Lightly grease a 25 cm (10 inch) loose-based round tart tin.

2 Roll out the pastry on a lightly floured work surface until 3 mm (⅛ inch) thick, to fit the base and side of the tin. Roll the pastry around the rolling pin, then lift and ease it into the tin, gently pressing to fit the side. Trim the edges, cover with plastic wrap and refrigerate for 30 minutes. Preheat the oven to 200°C (400°F/Gas 6).

3 Line the pastry shell with a crumpled piece of baking paper and cover the base with baking beads or uncooked rice. Bake the pastry for 20 minutes, then remove the paper and beads and bake for a further 10 minutes, or until the pastry is golden. Remove the pastry from the oven, then reduce the oven to 160°C (315°F/Gas 2–3).

4 Heat the olive oil in a large, heavy-based frying pan and add the onions. Cover and cook over low heat for 30 minutes, stirring often. The onions should be reduced in volume and golden in colour.

5 Spread the onions evenly over the pastry shell, crumble the goat's cheese over the onions, top with the tomato slices and sprinkle with the thyme. Whisk the egg yolks, eggs and cream in a bowl until smooth, season with salt and pepper, then pour over the tomato filling.

6 Bake for 30–40 minutes, or until filling has just set. Allow to cool slightly before serving warm or at room temperature.

Note: You could make this flan using blue cheese instead of goat's cheese, and sage instead of the thyme and rosemary.

ITALIAN EASTER PIE

SERVES 8

2 quantities shortcrust pastry (page 36)

1 tablespoon olive oil

100 g (3½ oz) Italian-style pork sausage, skin removed

1 garlic clove, chopped

¼ teaspoon chilli flakes

3 eggs, lightly beaten

500 g (1 lb 2 oz/2 cups) fresh ricotta cheese

60 g (2 oz) provolone cheese, grated

30 g (1 oz/scant ⅓ cup) parmesan cheese, finely grated

80 g (2¾ oz/½ cup) mozzarella cheese, grated

125 g (4 oz) prosciutto, thinly sliced

125 g (4 oz) mortadella, thinly sliced

2 tablespoons finely chopped flat-leaf (Italian) parsley

1 egg yolk

1 tablespoon milk

1 **Preheat the oven** to 180°C (350°F/Gas 4). Lightly grease a 24 cm (9½ inch) round spring-form cake tin.

2 **Using two-thirds** of the pastry, roll it out on a lightly floured work surface until 3 mm (⅛ inch) thick, to fit the base and side of the tin. Roll the pastry around the rolling pin, then lift and ease it into the tin, gently pressing to fit the side. Cover with plastic wrap and refrigerate for 30 minutes.

3 **Roll out the remaining pastry** until 3 mm (⅛ inch) thick, to fit the top of the tin. Put the pastry on a large plate, cover with plastic wrap and chill for 20 minutes.

4 **Line the pastry shell** with a crumpled piece of baking paper and cover the base with baking beads or uncooked rice. Bake the pastry for 10 minutes, then remove the paper and beads and bake for a further 20 minutes, or until the pastry is golden.

5 **Heat the olive oil** in a small frying pan over medium heat, add the sausage meat, garlic and chilli flakes and cook for 5 minutes, stirring to break up the meat. Set aside to cool.

6 **Combine the cooled** sausage mixture, eggs, ricotta, provolone, parmesan, mozzarella, prosciutto, mortadella and parsley in a bowl. Spoon into the pastry shell.

7 **Combine the egg yolk** with the milk and lightly brush the mixture over the edge of the pastry. Cover with the pastry round and gently press the edges to seal. Cut a small hole in the centre to allow steam to escape and brush the top with remaining egg mixture.

8 **Bake for 45 minutes**, or until the pastry is golden. Cool before serving.

WELSH LAMB PIE

SERVES 6

750 g (1 lb 10 oz) boned lamb shoulder, cubed

90 g (3 oz/¾ cup) plain (all-purpose) flour, seasoned

2 tablespoons olive oil

200 g (7 oz) bacon, finely chopped

2 garlic cloves, chopped

4 large leeks, sliced

1 large carrot, chopped

2 large potatoes, cut into 1 cm (½ inch) cubes

315 ml (10 fl oz/1¼ cups) beef stock

1 bay leaf

2 teaspoons chopped flat-leaf (Italian) parsley

375 g (13 oz) puff pastry

1 egg, lightly beaten

1 Toss the meat in the seasoned flour and shake off the excess. Heat the oil in a large frying pan over medium heat. Cook the meat in batches for 4-5 minutes, or until well browned, then remove from the pan.

2 Add the bacon and cook for 3 minutes. Add the garlic and leek and cook for about 5 minutes, or until the leek is soft.

3 Put the meat in a large saucepan, add the leek and bacon, carrot, potato, stock and bay leaf and bring to the boil, then reduce the heat, cover and simmer for 30 minutes. Uncover and simmer for 1 hour, or until the meat is cooked and the liquid thickened. Season. Remove the bay leaf, stir in the parsley and set aside to cool.

4 Preheat the oven to 200°C (400°F/Gas 6).

5 Divide filling among four 375 ml (1½ cup) pie dishes.

6 Divide the pastry into four and roll each piece out between two sheets of baking paper until large enough to cover the pie. Remove the top sheet of paper and invert the pastry over the filling. Trim the edges and pinch to seal. Cut two slits in the top for steam to escape. Brush with egg and bake for 45 minutes, or until the pastry is crisp and golden.

TRADITIONAL MEAT PIE

SERVES 4

750 g (1½ lb) gravy beef

40 g (1¼ oz/⅓ cup) plain flour

80 ml (2¾ fl oz/⅓ cup) oil

3 onions, sliced

500 ml (16 fl oz/2 cups) beef stock

1 tablespoon worcestershire sauce

2 tablespoons chopped parsley

1 sheet ready-rolled shortcrust pastry

1 sheet ready-rolled puff pastry

1 egg yolk, to glaze

1 Cut the beef into chunks. Season the flour with salt and freshly ground black pepper and place in a plastic bag. Add the meat and shake to coat with flour. Shake off any excess. Heat a little oil in a large heavy-based pan and cook meat, in batches, until golden brown. Remove from the pan.

2 Add the onion to the pan and cook over low heat until golden and translucent. Return the meat to the pan, add the stock and worcestershire sauce and stir well. Bring to the boil, then reduce the heat, cover and simmer gently for 2–2½ hours, or until the meat is very tender. You will need to stir the meat every 30 minutes to prevent sticking. Stir in the parsley. Remove from the pan and leave to cool completely, then refrigerate (preferably overnight).

3 Place a baking tray in the oven and preheat to 220°C (425°F/Gas 7).

4 Grease a deep 20 cm (8 inch) round pie plate. Use the shortcrust pastry to line the bottom and sides of the dish. You may need to roll the square of pastry a little larger to fit into prepared dish. Place cold filling in the pastry shell.

5 Mix the egg yolk with 2 teaspoons of water and use to brush the rim of the pastry shell. Place puff pastry over the top of the filling, press the edges gently to seal, then trim away the extra pastry. Pinch or crimp edges to decorate. Cut two small slits in the pastry to allow steam to escape during cooking. Brush with the beaten egg yolk mixture.

6 Place the pie on the preheated tray and bake for 20 minutes. Reduce heat to moderate 180°C (350°F/Gas 4) and cook for a further 15–20 minutes. Check pastry during cooking; if it is well browned, cover with a piece of foil for the remaining time.

SPINACH PIE

SERVES 4

450 g (1 lb) packet of frozen spinach, thawed

1 large sheet of frozen shortcrust (pie) pastry, thawed

3 garlic cloves, finely chopped

150 g (5½ oz) haloumi cheese, grated

125 g (4½ oz/heaped ¾ cup) crumbled feta

1 tablespoon oregano leaves

2 eggs

60 ml (2 fl oz/¼ cup) thick (double/heavy) cream

lemon wedges, to serve

1 Preheat the oven to 210°C (415°F/Gas 6–7).

2 Squeeze out the excess liquid from the spinach.

3 Place the pastry on a baking tray and spread the spinach in the middle, leaving a 3 cm (1¼ inch) border around the edge. Sprinkle the garlic over the spinach and pile the haloumi and feta on top. Sprinkle with the oregano and season well. Cut a short slit into each corner of the pastry, then tuck each side of the pastry over to form a border around the filling.

4 Lightly beat the eggs with the cream and carefully pour the egg mixture over the filling.

5 Bake for 30–40 minutes, or until the pastry is golden and the filling has set. Serve with the lemon wedges.

MOROCCAN CHICKEN FILO PIE

SERVES 4–6

1 tablespoon olive oil

1 red onion, chopped

2–3 cloves garlic, crushed

2 teaspoons grated fresh ginger

1 teaspoon ground turmeric

1 teaspoon ground cumin

1 teaspoon ground coriander

500 g (1 lb) cooked chicken, shredded

60 g (2 oz) slivered almonds, toasted

1 cup (50 g/1¾ oz) chopped coriander

20 g (¾ oz/⅓ cup) chopped parsley

1 teaspoon grated lemon rind

2 tablespoons stock or water

1 egg, lightly beaten

9 sheets filo pastry

60 g (2 oz) butter, melted

1 teaspoon caster sugar

¼ teaspoon ground cinnamon

1　Heat the oil in a large heavy-based frying pan and cook the onion, garlic and ginger, stirring, for 5 minutes, or until the onion is soft. Stir in the turmeric, cumin and coriander and cook, stirring, for 1–2 minutes. Remove from the heat, stir in the chicken, almonds, coriander, parsley and lemon rind. Leave to cool for 5 minutes, then stir in the stock or water and the beaten egg.

2　Preheat the oven to 180°C (350°F/Gas 4). Grease a baking tray.

3　Cut 6 sheets of filo into approximately 30 cm (12 inch) squares, retaining the extra strips. Cut each of the remaining sheets into 3 equal strips. Cover with a damp cloth.

4　Brush 1 square with the melted butter and place on the baking tray. Lay another square at an angle on top and brush with melted butter. Repeat with the other squares to form a rough 8-pointed star.

5　Spoon the chicken mixture into the centre, leaving a 5 cm (2 inch) border.

6　Turn the pastry edge in over the filling, leaving the centre open. Brush the pastry strips with melted butter, lightly scrunch them and lay them over the top of the pie. Sprinkle with the combined caster sugar and cinnamon.

7　Bake for 25 minutes, or until the pastry is cooked and golden brown.

GREAT TASTES BAKING

THAI THREE MUSHROOM TART

SERVES 8

375 g (13 oz) block of frozen puff pastry, thawed

1 teaspoon sesame oil

2 teaspoons vegetable oil

150 g (6 oz) shiitake mushrooms, trimmed

150 g (6 oz) button mushrooms, halved

150 g (6 oz) oyster mushrooms, halved

125 ml (4 fl oz/½ cup) coconut milk

1 lemongrass stem, white part only, chopped

1½ teaspoons grated fresh ginger

1 garlic clove, chopped

2 tablespoons chopped coriander (cilantro)

1 egg

1 tablespoon plain (all-purpose) flour

1 spring onion (scallion), sliced diagonally

1 Preheat the oven to 210°C (415°F/Gas 6–7). Grease a round, 25 cm (10 inch) loose-based flan (tart) tin, or a shallow 19 x 28 cm (7½ x 11¼ inch) rectangular one.

2 Roll out the pastry to line the base and sides of the tin and trim off any excess. Prick all over with a fork, then bake for 20 minutes, or until crisp. Leave to cool (gently press down the pastry if it has puffed too high). Reduce oven temperature to 200°C (400°F/Gas 6).

3 Heat the oils in a pan. Add the shiitake and button mushrooms and stir until lightly browned. Add the oyster mushrooms, then leave to cool. Pour away any liquid.

4 In a food processor, blend the coconut milk, lemon grass, ginger, garlic and coriander until fairly smooth. Add the egg and flour and blend in short bursts until combined. Season well.

5 Pour the mixture into the pastry case, top with the mushrooms and spring onion and bake for 30 minutes, or until the filling has set.

KANGAROO PIES

MAKES 4

FILLING

30 g (1 oz) butter

500 g (1 lb) kangaroo rump, cubed

2 rashers bacon, chopped

2 tablespoons plain flour

1 onion, chopped

2 carrots, chopped

2 sticks celery, chopped

125 g (4 oz) mushrooms, chopped

50 g (2 oz/⅓ cup) peas

250 ml (8 fl oz/1 cup) beef stock

1 tablespoon tomato paste

4 sheets ready-rolled puff pastry

1 egg yolk, lightly beaten, to glaze

1 **To make the filling,** heat the butter in a pan and cook the kangaroo and bacon, stirring, for 2 minutes, or until meat changes colour. Add flour and cook for 2–3 minutes, stirring, or until the flour has thickened slightly. Add the onion, carrot, celery, mushrooms, peas, stock and tomato paste. Reduce the heat and simmer for 1 hour, stirring frequently. Season to taste and set aside to cool.

2 **Grease four 12.5 cm** (4¾ inch) round pie tins. From each sheet of pastry, cut one 14 cm (5½ inch) diameter circle and one 12.5 cm (5 inch) diameter circle. Roll the larger circles to 16 cm (6½ inch) diameter and fit into the tins. Trim any excess pastry.

3 **Spoon a quarter** of the meat mixture into each. Mix the egg yolk with 1 teaspoon of water and brush the rims. Use the smaller circles to make the lids. Press the edges to seal and decorate with the prongs of a fork. Use any pastry scraps to decorate the pie tops and make a few slits to allow steam to escape.

4 **Place the pies** on an oven tray. Cover and refrigerate for at least 20 minutes.

5 **Preheat the oven** to 200°C (400°F/Gas 6). Brush the pastry with the egg yolk and water. Bake for 10 minutes, reduce the temperature to moderate 180°C (350°F/Gas 4) and bake for a further 20 minutes, or until puffed and golden brown.

TOMATO AND BACON QUICHE

SERVES 6

185 g (6 oz/1½ cups) plain flour, sifted

pinch of cayenne pepper

pinch of mustard powder

125 g (4 oz) cold butter, chopped

30 g (1 oz/⅓ cup) cheddar cheese, grated

1 egg yolk

FILLING

30 g (1 oz) butter

125 g (4 oz) bacon, rind and excess fat removed, chopped

1 small onion, finely sliced

3 eggs

185 ml (6 fl oz/¾ cup) cream

½ teaspoon salt

2 tomatoes, peeled, seeded and chopped into chunks

90 g (3 oz/¾ cup) mature cheddar cheese, grated

1 Process the flour, pepper, mustard and butter until crumbly. Add the cheese and egg yolk and process in short bursts until the mixture comes together. Add 1–2 tablespoons of water if needed. Turn out onto a floured surface and gather into a ball. Cover with plastic wrap and refrigerate for 30 minutes.

2 Grease a 3.5 cm (1½ inch) deep loose-based flan tin measuring 22 cm (8¾ inches) across the base.

3 To make the filling, melt the butter in a frying pan and cook the bacon for a few minutes over medium heat until golden. Add onion and cook until soft. Remove from heat.

4 Lightly beat the eggs, cream and salt in a bowl. Add the bacon and onion, then fold in the tomato and cheddar.

5 Roll out the pastry on a floured surface and fit into the tin. Place in the refrigerator for 30 minutes.

6 Preheat the oven to 180°C (350°F/Gas 4). Cover the pastry shell with baking paper and fill with baking beads. Bake for 10 minutes. Remove the paper and beads and bake for a further 10 minutes.

7 Pour the filling into the pastry shell and bake for 35 minutes, or until golden.

FIG AND APPLE PIES WITH ROSE WATER CREAM

SERVES 4

ROSE WATER CREAM

125 ml (4 fl oz/½ cup) thick (double/
heavy) cream

2 teaspoons of rosewater

1 tablespoon caster (superfine) sugar

---

3 apples, peeled, cored, and cut into
    2.5 cm (1 inch) cubes

3 fresh figs, or 6 semi-dried, cut into
    2 cm (¾ inch) cubes

3 tablespoons of unsalted butter

65 g (2 oz/¼ cup) caster (superfine)
    sugar

1 orange, zest grated

1 lemon, zest grated

juice of ½ lemon

1 cinnamon stick

1 teaspoon natural vanilla extract

1 sheet of store-bought shortcrust
    pastry

1 egg white, beaten, at room
    temperature

1   To make the rosewater cream, beat the cream,
rose water and sugar in a bowl until thick. Refrigerate
until needed.

2   Put the apples, figs, butter, sugar, orange zest, lemon zest,
lemon juice, cinnamon stick, vanilla, and 2 tablespoons water
in a saucepan. Stir over high heat until the butter has melted
and the sugar has dissolved. Bring to a boil, then reduce the
heat and simmer for 10 minutes, or until the apple is soft.
Remove from the heat and set aside to cool.

3   Preheat the oven to 180°C (350°F/Gas 4) and lightly grease
for 125 ml (4 f oz/ ½ cup) ovenproof ramekins.

4   Pour the cooled apple mixture into the ramekins,
discarding the cinnamon stick. Cut out four rounds of pastry
½ inch wider than the diameter of the ramekins. Lay the pastry
rounds over the ramekins, pressing around the rims to seal.
Brush the pastry with the egg white.

5   Bake the pies for 40 minutes, or until golden brown.
Serve warm with the rosewater cream

BERRY RICOTTA CREAM TARTLETS

SERVES 6

PASTRY

185 g (6 oz/1½ cups) plain flour

95 g (3 oz/1 cup) ground almonds

40 g (1 oz/⅓ cup) icing (confectioners')
sugar

125 g (4 oz) unsalted butter, chopped

1 egg, lightly beaten

FILLING

200 g (7 oz/¾ cup) ricotta cheese

1 teaspoon vanilla essence

2 eggs

160 g (5½ oz/⅔ cup) caster (superfine)
sugar

125 ml (4 fl oz/½ cup) cream

60 g (2 oz/½ cup) raspberries

90 g (3 oz/½ cup) blueberries

icing (confectioners') sugar, to dust

1   Sift the flour into a bowl. Add the almonds and icing sugar. Rub the butter into the flour with your fingertips until it resembles breadcrumbs. Make a well in the centre, add the egg and mix with a flat-bladed knife, using a cutting action, until the mixture comes together in beads. Gather the dough and put onto a lightly floured surface. Press into a ball, cover with plastic wrap and refrigerate for 30 minutes.

2   Grease six 8 cm x 3 cm deep (3¼ x 1⅛ inch) loose bottomed tart tins.

3   Divide the pastry into six and roll each piece out between two sheets of baking paper to fit the base and side of the tins. Press the pastry into the tins, trim the edges and prick the bases with a fork. Refrigerate for 30 minutes.

4   Preheat the oven to 180°C (350°F/Gas 4). Line the pastry with crumpled baking paper and spread with baking beads or rice. Bake for 8-10 minutes, then remove the paper and beads.

5   Process the ricotta, vanilla, eggs, sugar and cream in a food processor until smooth.

6   Divide the berries and filling among the tarts and bake for 25-30 minutes, or until the filling is just set — the top should be soft but not too wobbly. Cool. Dust with a little icing sugar and serve.

ROASTED PUMPKIN, GARLIC AND PECORINO PIE

SERVES 6–8

OLIVE OIL PASTRY

375 g (13 oz/3 cups) plain
  (all-purpose) flour

1 teaspoon sea salt

125 ml (4 fl oz/½ cup) extra
  virgin olive oil

1 egg, lightly beaten

ROASTED PUMPKIN FILLING

1.5 kg (3 lb 5 oz) jap (kent) pumpkin,
  peeled, seeded and cut into
  2 cm (¾ inch) pieces

6 garlic cloves, unpeeled

60 ml (2 fl oz/¼ cup) olive oil

3 eggs, lightly beaten

100 g (3½ oz/1 cup) grated pecorino
  cheese

2 teaspoons chopped marjoram

½ teaspoon freshly grated nutmeg

sea salt

1 **To make the olive oil pastry,** combine the flour and sea salt in a large bowl and make a well in the centre. Combine the olive oil, egg and 80 ml (2 ½ fl oz/⅓ cup) cold water in a small bowl and whisk to mix well. Pour oil mixture into the well, then, using a fork, stir to combine and to form a coarse dough. Add 1–2 tablespoons extra water, if necessary. Turn out dough onto work surface. Knead for 3 minutes, or until smooth. Wrap dough in plastic wrap. Refrigerate for 2 hours.

2 **Preheat the oven** to 200°C (400°F/Gas 6).

3 **To make the roasted pumpkin filling,** put the pumpkin and unpeeled garlic cloves in a large roasting tin, drizzle with olive oil and toss to coat. Roast for 30 minutes, or until the pumpkin and garlic are tender. When cool enough to handle, squeeze the garlic from the skins. Using a fork, mash the garlic and pumpkin, then stir in the eggs, pecorino, marjoram and nutmeg. Season with sea salt and freshly ground black pepper.

Reduce the oven to 190°C (375°F/Gas 5). Grease a 16 x 26 cm (6¼ x 10½ inch) rectangular shallow tin.

4 **Using two-thirds of the pastry,** roll out on a floured work surface to 2 mm (¹⁄₁₆ inch) thick, to fit the base and side of the tin, the pastry will not cover the sides all the way to the top. Cover with plastic wrap and refrigerate for 30 minutes.

5 **Spoon in the filling,** smoothing it even.

6 **Roll out the remaining pastry** on a floured surface, and cut into 2 cm (¾ inch) wide strips, long enough to fit diagonally across the pie. Position the pastry strips across the top of the pie, spacing them 1 cm (½ inch) apart, and trim the ends to neaten.

7 **Bake** for 1 hour, or until the pastry is crisp and golden. Serve the pie warm or at room temperature.

CUMIN AND GOUDA GOUGERES

MAKES 40

100 g (3½ oz) butter

140 g (5 oz) plain (all-purpose) flour

½ teaspoon cumin seeds, lightly crushed

3 eggs

150 g (6 oz) aged gouda cheese, finely grated

1 Preheat the oven to 200°C (400°F/Gas 6). Line a baking tray with baking paper.

2 Heat 250 ml (9 fl oz/1 cup) water, the butter and ¼ teaspoon salt in a small saucepan over medium heat until butter has melted and the mixture has just come to the boil. Add the flour and cumin and stir until the mixture comes away from the side of the saucepan. Transfer to the bowl of an electric mixer and allow to cool a little (alternatively use a hand mixer or wooden spoon). Beating continuously, add the eggs one at a time, beating well after each addition. Stir in the cheese.

3 Put teaspoonfuls of the mixture onto the prepared baking tray, spacing them about 4 cm (1½ inches) apart.

4 Bake for 20 minutes, then reduce the heat to 160°C (315°F/Gas 2–3) and cook for a further 20 minutes, or until the gougères are puffed, golden and dry. Turn off the oven, open the door slightly and leave the gougères to cool a little.

5 Serve warm or at room temperature, with drinks.

Note: Gougères originated in Burgundy, traditionally as an accompaniment to the local wines. They can also be split and filled with savoury fillings, such as chicken or fish.

COCONUT BAKLAVA

MAKES 24

360 g (12¾ oz/4 cups) desiccated coconut

1 teaspoon ground cinnamon

½ teaspoon ground nutmeg

a pinch of ground cloves

10 sheets filo pastry (about 150 g/5½ oz)

200 g (7 oz) unsalted butter, melted

SYRUP

400 g (14 oz/1¾ cups) caster (superfine) sugar

1½ tablespoons lemon juice

1½ tablespoons honey

1 tablespoon orange blossom water

1 Preheat the oven to 180°C (350°F/Gas 4). Lightly grease a 28 x 20 cm (11¼ x 8 inch) rectangular shallow tin and line the base with baking paper.

2 Put the coconut, cinnamon, nutmeg and cloves in a large bowl and stir to combine.

3 Cut the stack of filo sheets in half widthways, so it will fit into the tin. Brush a sheet of filo liberally with melted butter, top with another sheet and repeat until you have four layers of pastry. Repeat with the remaining filo to give five stacks in total, each with four layers.

4 Put one stack of filo in the tin and brush the top of the filo with butter. Evenly spread one-quarter of the coconut mixture over the filo, top with another filo stack and brush with butter. Repeat with remaining coconut mixture and pastry stacks, finishing with a layer of filo. Liberally brush the top with butter,

then score into diamond shapes using a sharp knife, making the cuts about 1 cm (½ inch) deep (do not cut all the way through at this stage).

5 Bake for 18–20 minutes, or until golden and crisp.

6 Meanwhile, make the syrup. Combine 400 ml (14 fl oz) water, the sugar, lemon juice, honey and orange blossom water in a saucepan and stir until the sugar dissolves. Bring to a simmer and cook for 10 minutes, or until slightly thickened. Cool the syrup.

7 While the baklava is still very hot, pour over the cold syrup. Allow to cool completely before cutting along the scored marks into diamond shapes to serve.

PALM SUGAR, LIME AND STAR ANISE COILS

MAKES 24

2 star anise

60 g (2 oz) palm sugar (jaggery), finely grated, or soft brown sugar

2 teaspoons lime zest

2 sheets ready-rolled frozen butter puff pastry, thawed

40 g (1½ oz) butter, melted

1 Preheat the oven to 200°C (400°F/Gas 6). Line a baking tray with baking paper.

2 Put the star anise in a small ovenproof dish and dry-roast in the oven for 5 minutes. Cool, then grind using a mortar and pestle to form a fine powder. Mix together the ground anise, palm sugar and lime zest in a small bowl.

3 Lay the two sheets of pastry on the work surface and brush each with some of the melted butter. Scatter the palm sugar mixture over the two sheets. Take one pastry sheet and roll it up firmly to form a long log. Repeat with the second pastry sheet. Cut each log into 12 even-sized slices, then put the slices on the baking tray, spacing them a little apart. Flatten each pastry slightly with the palm of your hand, then brush the tops with the remaining butter. Refrigerate for 30 minutes, then bake for 20 minutes, or until puffed and golden brown.

Note: You could also use a clean coffee grinder to grind the roasted star anise.

PEACH GALETTES

MAKES 12

2 quantities sweet shortcrust pastry (page 36)

600 g (1 lb 5 oz) peaches, stoned and thinly sliced

30 g (1 oz) butter, melted

1 tablespoon honey

1 tablespoon caster (superfine) sugar

¼ teaspoon ground nutmeg

1 egg yolk

1 tablespoon milk

3 tablespoons apricot jam

25 g (1 oz/¼ cup) flaked almonds, toasted

1 Lightly grease a baking tray or line it with baking paper.

2 Roll out the pastry on a lightly floured work surface to 3 mm (⅛ inch) thick. Cut out twelve 12 cm (4 ½ inch) rounds.

3 Gently toss together the peach slices, butter, honey, sugar and nutmeg in a bowl. Divide the peach mixture between the pastry rounds, leaving a 1 cm (½ inch) border around the edge. Fold the pastry over the filling, leaving the centre uncovered, pleating the pastry at 1 cm (½ inch) intervals to fit. Place the galettes on the tray and refrigerate for 30 minutes.

4 Meanwhile, preheat the oven to 200°C (400°F/Gas 6).

5 Combine the egg yolk and milk in a small bowl to make a glaze. Brush the glaze over the edges of the pastry. Bake for 30 minutes, or until golden.

6 Combine the apricot jam and 1 tablespoon water in a small saucepan and stir over low heat until smooth. Brush the jam mixture over the hot galettes, then sprinkle with almonds. Cool before serving.

GINGER AND MANGO ÉCLAIRS

MAKES 16

1 quantity choux pastry (see page 37)

1 x 5 g (⅛ oz) gelatine sheet, or
   1½ teaspoons gelatine powder

200 ml (7 fl oz) puréed mango flesh

1 teaspoon lemon juice

125 ml (4 fl oz/½ cup) thick (double/
   heavy) cream

30 g (1 oz/¼ cup) icing
   (confectioners') sugar

GINGER ICING

60 g (2¼ oz/½ cup) icing
   (confectioners') sugar

10 g (¼ oz) unsalted butter

½ teaspoon ground ginger

½ teaspoon lemon juice

1 **Preheat the oven** to 200°C (400°F/Gas 6). Line two baking trays with baking paper.

2 **Put the choux pastry** into a piping bag fitted with a 2 cm (¾ inch) plain nozzle. Pipe 10 cm (4 inch) lengths of choux onto the baking tray, spacing them 4 cm (1 ½ inches) apart.

3 **Bake for 20 minutes,** then reduce the heat to 160°C (315°F/Gas 2–3) and bake for another 20 minutes, or until puffed, golden and dry. Turn off the oven, open the door slightly and leave the choux in the oven until cool.

4 **If using the gelatine sheet,** soak it in cold water for 5 minutes, or until softened, then squeeze out excess moisture. If using gelatine powder, sprinkle gelatine over 3 tablespoons water in a bowl. Leave the gelatine to sponge — it will swell.

5 **Combine the mango purée** and lemon juice in a small heatproof bowl over simmering water. Add the softened gelatine sheet or sponged gelatine powder to the warm liquid, whisking to dissolve the gelatine. Remove from the heat, then refrigerate until the mixture is cool and beginning to thicken.

6 **Whisk the cream** and icing sugar in a bowl until thick, then fold in the cooled mango mixture.

7 **To make the ginger icing,** combine the icing sugar, butter, ginger and lemon juice in a small bowl. Pour over 2 teaspoons boiling water. Whisk until a smooth, thin icing forms, adding a few more drops of water if necessary.

8 **Without cutting all the way** through, split the éclairs horizontally. Spoon about 1 tablespoon of filling into each. Drizzle the tops with ginger icing. Refrigerate until icing sets.

PORTUGUESE CUSTARD TARTS

SERVES 4

155 g (5½ oz/1¼ cups) plain (all-purpose) flour

25 g (1 oz) Copha (white vegetable shortening), chopped and softened

30 g (1 oz) unsalted butter, chopped and softened

250 g (9 oz/1 cup) sugar

500 ml (17 fl oz/2 cups) milk

3 tablespoons cornflour (cornstarch)

1 tablespoon custard powder

4 egg yolks

1 teaspoon natural vanilla extract

1   Sift the flour into a bowl. Add 185 ml (6 fl oz/¾ cup) water, or enough to form a soft dough. Gather into a ball, then roll out on baking paper to form a 24 x 30 cm (9 ½ in x 12 in) rectangle. Spread the Copha over the surface. Roll up from the short edge to form a log.

2   Roll the dough out into a rectangle again, and spread with the butter. Roll into a log and slice into 12 pieces. Working from the centre outwards, use your fingertips to press each round out to a circle large enough to cover the base and sides of twelve 80 ml (2½ fl oz/⅓ cup) muffin holes. Press into tin. Refrigerate.

3   Put the sugar and 80 ml (2½ fl oz/⅓ cup) water into a pan, and stir over low heat until the sugar dissolves. Mix a little milk with the cornflour and custard powder to form a smooth paste, and add to the pan with the remaining milk, egg yolks and vanilla. Stir over low heat until thickened. Put in a bowl, cover and cool.

4   Preheat the oven to 220°C (425°F/Gas 7).

5   Divide the filling among the pastry bases. Bake for 30 minutes, or until the custard is set and the tops have browned. Cool in the tins, then transfer to a wire rack.

OLD-FASHIONED APPLE PIE

SERVES 8

PASTRY

250 g (9 oz/2 cups) self-raising flour

85 g (3 oz/⅔ cup) cornflour (cornstarch)

180 g (6½ oz) unsalted butter, chilled
and cubed

90 g (3¼ oz/⅓ cup) caster (superfine)
sugar

1 egg, lightly beaten

40 g (1½ oz) unsalted butter

6 green apples, peeled, cored and
thinly sliced

1 tablespoon lemon juice

140 g (5 oz/¾ cup) soft brown sugar

1 teaspoon ground nutmeg

2 tablespoons plain (all-purpose) flour
mixed with
60 ml (2 fl oz/¼ cup) water

25 g (1 oz/¼ cup) ground almonds

milk, to brush

sugar, to sprinkle

1   Lightly grease a 1 litre, (35 fl oz/4 cups) 20 cm (8 in) metal pie dish.

2   Sift the flours into a large bowl and rub in the butter with your fingers until the mixture resembles fine breadcrumbs. Stir in the sugar and a pinch of salt. Make a well, add the egg and mix with a knife, using a cutting action, until the mixture comes together in beads. Put the dough on a floured surface and press into a smooth disc, cover with plastic wrap and refrigerate for 20 minutes.

3   Use two-thirds of the dough to line the base and side of the dish. Roll out the remaining dough to make a lid. Cover and refrigerate for 20 minutes. Preheat the oven to 200°C (400°F/Gas 6) and heat a baking tray.

4   Melt the butter in a large frying pan, add the apple and toss. Stir in the lemon juice, sugar and nutmeg and cook for 10 minutes, or until tender. Add the flour and water mixture, then the almonds. Bring to the boil and cook, stirring, for 2–3 minutes. Pour into a bowl and cool.

5   Put the apple in the pastry case. Cover with the pastry lid and press lightly onto the rim. Trim the edges and pinch together to seal. Prick over the top, brush with milk and sprinkle with sugar.

6   Bake on the hot tray for 40 minutes, or until golden.

FREEFORM BLUEBERRY PIE

SERVES 6–8

PASTRY

185 g (6½ oz/1½ cups) plain (all-purpose) flour

100 g (3½ oz) unsalted butter, chilled and cubed

2 teaspoons grated orange zest

1 tablespoon caster (superfine) sugar

2–3 tablespoons iced water

40 g (1½ oz/⅓ cup) crushed amaretti biscuits or almond bread

60 g (2¼ oz/½ cup) plain (all-purpose) flour

1 teaspoon ground cinnamon

90 g (3¼ oz/⅓ cup) caster (superfine) sugar

500 g (1 lb 2 oz/3¼ cups) fresh blueberries

milk, for brushing

2 tablespoons blueberry jam

icing (confectioners') sugar, to dust

1 Sift the flour into a large bowl and rub in the butter with your fingertips until the mixture resembles breadcrumbs. Stir in the orange zest and sugar. Make a well, add almost all the water and mix with a flat-bladed knife, using a cutting action, until the mixture comes together in beads. Add a little more water if necessary to bring the dough together. Gather together and lift out onto a lightly floured surface. Press together into a ball and flatten it slightly into a disc. Cover in plastic wrap and refrigerate for 20 minutes.

2 Preheat the oven to 200°C (400°F/Gas 6).

3 Combine the crushed biscuits, flour, cinnamon and 1½ tablespoons of the sugar.

4 Roll the pastry out to a 36 cm (14¼ in) circle and sprinkle with the biscuit mixture, leaving a 4 cm (1½ in) border. Arrange the blueberries over the crushed biscuits, then bring up the edges to form a freeform crust.

5 Brush the sides of the pie with the milk. Sprinkle with the remaining sugar and bake for 30 minutes, or until the sides are crisp and brown.

6 Warm the jam in a saucepan over low heat and brush over the berries. Cool to room temperature, then dust the pastry crust with sifted icing sugar.

MANGO AND PASSIONFRUIT PIES

MAKES 6

750 g ready-made or home-made
   sweet shortcrust pastry (see page 36)

3 ripe mangoes (900 g), peeled and
   sliced or chopped, or 400 g tin
   mango slices, drained

60 g (2¼ oz/¼ cup) passionfruit pulp,
   strained

1 tablespoon custard powder

90 g (3¼ oz/⅓ cup) caster
   (superfine) sugar

1 egg, lightly beaten

icing (confectioners') sugar, to dust

1 **Preheat the oven** to 190°C (375°F/Gas 5). Grease six 10 cm (top) 8 cm (3¼ in) (base) 3 cm (1¼ in) (deep) fluted flan tins or round pie dishes.

2 **Roll out two-thirds** of the pastry between two sheets of baking paper to a thickness of 3 mm (⅛ in). Cut out six 13 cm (5 in) circles. Line the tins with the circles and trim the edges. Refrigerate while you make the filling.

3 **Combine the mango,** passionfruit, custard powder and sugar in a bowl.

4 **Roll out the remaining pastry** between two sheets of baking paper to 3 mm (⅛ in) thick. Cut out six 11 cm (4¼ in) circles. Re-roll the pastry trimmings and cut into shapes for decoration.

5 **Fill the pastry cases** with the mango mixture and brush the edges with egg. Top with the pastry circles and press the edges to seal. Trim the edges and decorate with the pastry shapes. Brush the tops with beaten egg and dust with icing sugar.

6 **Bake for 20–25 minutes,** or until the pastry is golden brown. Delicious served with cream.

RAISIN PIE

SERVES 6–8

600 g ready-made or home-made
  sweet shortcrust pastry (see page 36)

80 ml (2½ fl oz/⅓ cup) orange juice

2 tablespoons lemon juice

320 g (11¼ oz/2½ cups) raisins

140 g (5 oz/¾ cup) soft brown sugar

½ teaspoon mixed (pumpkin pie) spice

30 g (1 oz/¼ cup) cornflour (cornstarch)

1 teaspoon finely grated lemon zest

1 teaspoon finely grated orange zest

1 egg, lightly beaten

1 tablespoon sugar, to sprinkle

1 **Preheat the oven** to 190°C (375°F/Gas 5). Heat a baking tray. Grease a 23 cm (9 inch) pie tin.

2 **Roll out two-thirds** of the pastry between two sheets of baking paper to fit the base and side of the dish. Remove the top paper and invert the pastry into the tin, pressing it into the tin. Trim the excess. Chill the base and remaining pastry.

3 **Combine the citrus juices,** raisins and 250 ml (8 fl oz/ 1 cup) water in a pan. Boil over high heat, stirring occasionally, for 2 minutes. Remove from the heat.

4 **Mix the brown sugar,** mixed spice and cornflour in a bowl. Add 125 ml (4 fl oz/½ cup) water and mix until smooth. Slowly stir into raisin mixture and return the pan to the stove over high heat. Boil, stirring, then reduce to a simmer, stirring occasionally, for 5 minutes, or until it thickens. Stir in the citrus zest and cool for 30 minutes.

5 **Roll out the remaining pastry** to cover the pie. Fill base with raisin mixture, brush the edges with the egg and cover with the pastry top. Pinch the edges together and make a few small holes. Brush with egg, sprinkle with sugar and bake for 40 minutes, or until golden. Serve warm or cold.

INDIVIDUAL LEMON AND PASSIONFRUIT TARTS

SERVES 6

60 g (2¼ oz) unsalted butter

90 g (3¼ oz/⅓ cup) caster (superfine) sugar

2 eggs

2 tablespoons self-raising flour, sifted

60 ml (2 fl oz/¼ cup) lemon juice

1 teaspoon grated lemon zest

1 passionfruit, pulp removed

3 sheets filo pastry

125 g (5 oz/1 cup) fresh raspberries

whipped cream, to serve

1 **Preheat the oven** to 180°C (350°F/Gas 4).

2 **Beat the butter** and caster sugar until light and creamy. Add the eggs one at a time, beating well after each addition. Add the flour, lemon juice, zest and passionfruit pulp and beat until well combined.

3 **Fold each sheet** of filo pastry in half from the short end up. Fold again and cut in half. Carefully line six 125 ml (½ cup) muffin holes with a piece of pastry.

4 **Pour in the lemon mixture** and bake for 20–25 minutes, or until set.

5 **Serve topped** with fresh raspberries and, if desired, whipped cream.

NASHI AND GINGER STRUDEL

SERVES 6–8

4 small nashi pears, peeled, cored and sliced

1 tablespoon lemon juice

2 teaspoons fresh ginger, finely grated

30 g (1 oz/½ cup) panko (Japanese breadcrumbs)

230 g (8 oz/1 cup) caster (superfine) sugar

40 g (1½ oz/¼ cup) sesame seeds, lightly toasted, plus extra to garnish

50 g (1¾ oz/½ cup) walnuts, very finely chopped

1½ teaspoons ground cinnamon

1 teaspoon ground ginger

8 sheets filo pastry

150 g (6 oz) unsalted butter, melted

2 tablespoons icing (confectioners') sugar

2 tablespoons kinako (roasted soya bean flour)

ice cream, to serve

1 **Preheat the oven to 180°C** (350°F/Gas 4). Lightly grease a baking tray.

2 **Put the nashi slices** in a bowl with the lemon juice, fresh ginger, panko and half the sugar and stir well.

3 **Combine the sesame seeds,** walnuts, cinnamon, ground ginger and remaining sugar in a separate bowl.

4 **Lay one sheet of filo** on a work surface with the long edge towards you, brush lightly with melted butter, then lay another sheet on top so it overlaps the edge furthest away from you by about 5 cm (2 in). Brush on a little more butter.

5 **Sprinkle about one-quarter** of the sesame mixture over the top of the two pastry sheets, then keep layering in the same position with the rest of the filo and sesame mix, brushing each sheet of pastry with melted butter. Leave a 4 cm (1½ in) border along the edge of the pastry closest to you and on both sides, and place nashi mixture in a neat log along the edge closest to you. Carefully roll up, folding in the sides about halfway along. Continue rolling to the end.

6 **Carefully transfer** the strudel to the prepared tray, seam side down, and brush all over with melted butter. Bake for 50 minutes, or until golden.

7 **Allow to cool slightly** before sprinkling with sifted combined icing sugar and kinako.

8 **Slice on the diagonal** and serve with lightly whipped cream, if desired.

BLACKBERRY PIE

SERVES 6

500 g ready-made or home-made
   sweet shortcrust pastry (see page 36)

500 g (1 lb 2 oz/4 cups) blackberries

160 g (5½ oz/⅔ cup) caster
   (superfine) sugar

2 tablespoons cornflour (cornstarch)

milk, to brush

1 egg, lightly beaten

caster (superfine) sugar, extra, to sprinkle

cream or ice cream, to serve

1 **Preheat the oven** to 200°C (400°F/Gas 6). Grease a 26 cm (10½ inch) deep ceramic pie dish.

2 **Roll out two-thirds** of the pastry between two sheets of baking paper until large enough to line the base and side of the pie dish. Remove the top paper, invert the pastry into the dish and press firmly into place, leaving the excess overhanging the edges.

3 **Toss the blackberries** (if frozen, thaw and drain well), sugar and cornflour together in a bowl until well mixed, then transfer to the pie dish.

4 **Roll out the remaining pastry** between two sheets of baking paper until large enough to cover the pie. Moisten the rim of the pie base with milk and press the pastry lid firmly into place. Trim and crimp the edges. Brush with egg and sprinkle with the extra sugar. Pierce the top of the pie with a knife.

5 **Bake on the bottom shelf** of the oven for 10 minutes. Reduce the oven to 180°C (350°F/Gas 4) and move the pie to the centre shelf. Bake for another 30 minutes, or until golden on top. Cool before serving with cream or ice cream.

KEY LIME PIE

SERVES 6–8

375 g (13 oz) ready-made or home-made sweet shortcrust pastry (see page 36)

4 egg yolks

395 g (13¾ oz) tin condensed milk

125 ml (4 fl oz/½ cup) lime juice

2 teaspoons grated lime zest

lime slices, to garnish

icing (confectioners') sugar, to dust

whipped cream, to serve

1   **Preheat the oven** to 180°C (350°F/Gas 4). Grease a 23 cm (9 inch) loose-bottomed flan tin.

2   **Roll the dough** out between two sheets of baking paper until it is large enough to fit into the pie tin. Remove the top sheet of paper and invert the pastry into the tin. Use a small ball of pastry to help press the pastry into the tin, allowing any excess to hang over the sides. Use a small sharp knife to trim away any extra pastry.

3   **Line the pastry shell** with a piece of crumpled baking paper that is large enough to cover the base and side of the tin and pour in some baking beads or rice. Bake for 10 minutes, remove the paper and beads and return the pastry to the oven for another 4–5 minutes, or until the base is dry. Leave to cool.

4   **Using electric beaters**, beat the egg yolks, condensed milk, lime juice and zest in a large bowl for 2 minutes, or until well combined. Pour into the pie shell and smooth the surface.

5   **Bake for 20–25 minutes**, or until set. Allow the pie to cool, then refrigerate for 2 hours, or until well chilled. Garnish with lime slices, dust with sifted icing sugar and serve with whipped cream.

ALMOND PIES

MAKES 8

50 g (1¾ oz/½ cup) flaked almonds

125 g (4½ oz) unsalted butter, softened

125 g (4½ oz/1 cup) icing (confectioners') sugar

125 g (4½ oz/1¼ cups) ground almonds

30 g (1 oz/¼ cup) plain (all-purpose) flour

2 eggs

1 tablespoon rum or brandy

1 teaspoon almond extract

½ teaspoon natural vanilla extract

4 sheets frozen ready-made puff pastry, thawed

1 egg, lightly beaten

sugar, to sprinkle

icing (confectioners') sugar, to dust

1 **Preheat the oven** to 200°C (400°F/Gas 6).

2 **Bake the flaked almonds** on a baking tray for 2–3 minutes, or until just golden. Remove and return the tray to the oven to keep it hot.

3 **Beat together the butter,** icing sugar, ground almonds, flour, eggs, rum, almond essence and vanilla with electric beaters for 2–3 minutes, or until smooth and combined. Fold in the flaked almonds.

4 **Cut out eight** 10 cm (4 in) rounds and another eight 11 cm (4¼ in) rounds from the puff pastry.

5 **Spread the smaller rounds** with equal amounts of filling, leaving a 1 cm border. Brush the borders with beaten egg and cover with the tops. Seal the edges with a fork and, if you wish, decorate the tops with shapes cut from pastry scraps. Pierce with a fork to allow steam to escape. Brush with egg and sprinkle with sugar.

6 **Bake on the hot tray** for 15–20 minutes, or until the pastry is puffed and golden. Dust with icing sugar before serving.

COOKIES

COOKIES BASICS

Nothing beats the heavenly aroma of freshly baked biscuits. Biscuits are made using several methods, each giving special characteristics to the biscuits.

In biscuit-making, the recipe needs to be followed exactly, so make sure you follow the method and weigh the ingredients carefully. Even so, biscuits aren't supposed to be perfect — they just need to be fun to make and delicious to eat.

CREAMING METHOD: With the following recipe, you can make a basic butter biscuit and variations. To make about 30 biscuits, line two trays with baking paper or lightly grease with melted butter. Soften 125 g (4½ oz) butter, then cut into cubes.

Preheat the oven to 210°C (415°F/Gas 6–7). Cream the softened butter with 125 g (4½ oz/½ cup) caster (superfine) sugar in a bowl using electric beaters until light and fluffy. The mixture should be pale and smooth. The sugar should be almost dissolved. Add 60 ml (2 fl oz/¼ cup) milk and ¼ teaspoon natural vanilla extract and beat until combined. Add 185 g (6 oz/1½ cups) self-raising flour and 60 g (2¼ oz/½ cup) custard powder (instant vanilla pudding mix) and use a flat-bladed knife to bring to a soft dough. Rotate the bowl as you work and use a cutting motion to incorporate the dry ingredients. Don't overwork the dough.

Roll level teaspoonfuls into balls and place on the trays, leaving 5 cm (2 in) between each biscuit. Flatten the balls lightly with your fingertips, then press with a fork. The biscuits should be about 5 cm (2 in) in diameter.

Bake for 15–18 minutes, until lightly golden. Cool on the trays for 3 minutes before transferring to a wire rack to cool completely. Store in an airtight container for up to a week.

To freeze, place in freezer bags and seal, label and date. Unfilled and un-iced cooked biscuits can be frozen for up to two months. After thawing, refresh them in a 180°C (350°F/Gas 4) oven for a few minutes, then cool and decorate, as desired, before serving. Uncooked biscuit dough freezes well. To do this, wrap it in plastic wrap, place in a plastic bag and seal. When ready to use, thaw at room temperature and bake as directed.

Plain cooked biscuits can be decorated with icing (confectioners') sugar just before serving. Or they can be iced, or drizzled with melted chocolate.

Variations

CITRUS: Omit the natural vanilla extract, add 2 teaspoons orange or lemon zest to the creamed butter and sugar and proceed with the recipe. When cool, combine 250 g (9 oz/2 cups) sifted icing (confectioners') sugar, 20 g (¾ oz) softened butter and 1 tablespoon lemon or orange juice in a bowl and ice the biscuits.

NUTTY: Mix 55 g (2 oz/½ cup) finely chopped walnuts or pecans into the basic mixture before adding the flour. Press a nut onto each biscuit, instead of pressing with a fork, and bake as above.

Biscuits can also be made using the following methods:

MELT AND MIX: This quick method involves mixing the dry ingredients, then mixing in the melted butter (and any other ingredients in the recipe) with a wooden spoon until the dry ingredients are well moistened.

RUBBING IN: This involves cutting cold butter into pieces and rubbing it into the flour with your fingertips until the mixture is crumbly and resembles fine breadcrumbs. Then almost all the liquid is added and cut into the dry ingredients with a knife, adding the remaining liquid if necessary to bring the mixture together. Do not add the liquid all at once as flour varies a great deal so the full amount of liquid may not be required.

Perfect: Has even golden colouring on both the top and base and even thickness.

Unevenly spread: Mixture too close together on the tray or too wet.

Undercooked, sticking: Pale and soft indicates the cooking time was too short.

Hints and tips

- An electric hand mixer is very useful for whisking and creaming.

- Some recipes can be made using a food processor, however biscuit dough should not be overworked or an excess of gluten will develop, resulting in a tough biscuit. Only use a processor to rub the fat into the flour. When the liquid is added, pulse briefly until the mixture just comes together, then turn out onto a work surface to bring together into a smooth, soft ball, without kneading. Then cut or shape as directed.

- Always weigh and measure ingredients accurately.

- Make sure your ingredients are at the right temperature. Chilled butter means butter straight out of the refrigerator. Softened butter means butter returned to room temperature — this takes about 45 minutes. Eggs also need to be at room temperature. Remove them from the refrigerator about 45 minutes before using.

- Prepare baking trays as specified. Not all recipes require the tray to be greased or lined.

- Always preheat the oven to the required temperature and test with an oven thermometer.

- Make sure the oven shelves are set at an equal distance apart if cooking more than one tray at a time.

- Biscuits spread during baking, some more than others. Most average sized baking trays fit three rows of five biscuits, with the biscuit mixture spaced about 5 cm (2 inches) apart.

- Lightly flour the work surface and rolling pin before and during rolling if the dough starts to stick. Do not use excessive amounts of flour or it can affect the biscuit.

- If using a pastry cutter to stamp out shapes, dip the cutting edge into a little extra flour from time to time to prevent sticking.

- Biscuits can be baked on two trays at the same time, but often the tray underneath will require a longer cooking time. If you have time, cook the biscuits in batches. Alternatively, switch the trays halfway through cooking time.

- Always place biscuit dough onto a cold baking tray. If baking in batches, allow the tray to cool before adding the next batch.

- Always bake for the minimum time given and check for doneness. Cook for only 2 minutes more and then retest (biscuits can be underdone one minute and then burnt the next).

- Always cool biscuits on a wire cooling rack or they can become soggy. Allow biscuits to cool completely before icing or filling.

- Some biscuit recipes call for nuts, whether whole, chopped or ground. Nuts are often toasted before being ground. To toast nuts, put them in a single layer on a baking tray and bake in a preheated 180°C (350°F/Gas 4) oven for 5–10 minutes, depending on the type of nut or whether they are ground or whole. Always time this or keep a good check on them, as nuts are easy to burn.

Overcooked: Biscuits will continue to cook if left of the tray.

Too thick: Mixture was rolled and cut too thickly – will require extra baking time.

Too thin: Mixture was rolled to thinly or oven was too hot or time was too long.

MANDARIN WHIRLS

MAKES 18 'SANDWICHES'

350 g (12 oz) unsalted butter, softened

60 g (2¼ oz/½ cup) icing (confectioners') sugar

grated zest from 2 mandarins or 1 large orange

250 g (9 oz/2 cups) plain (all-purpose) flour

60 g (2¼ oz/½ cup) cornflour (cornstarch)

ICING

120 g (4¼ oz) unsalted butter, softened

250 g (9 oz/2 cups) icing (confectioners') sugar

2 tablespoons freshly squeezed mandarin or orange juice

1   Preheat the oven to 180°C (350°F/Gas 4). Line two baking trays with baking paper.

2   Cream the butter, icing sugar and zest in a bowl using electric beaters until pale and fluffy. Sift the flour and cornflour into the bowl, then stir with a wooden spoon until a soft dough forms.

3   Transfer the mixture to a piping bag fitted with a 4 cm (1½ inch) star nozzle and pipe thirty-six 4 cm (1 ½ inch) rounds, spacing them well apart on baking trays. Bake 12–15 minutes, or until lightly golden on the edges. Cool on the trays for 5 minutes, then transfer to a wire rack to cool completely.

4   To make the icing, using electric beaters, cream the butter, icing sugar and mandarin juice in a bowl until pale and soft. Use the icing to sandwich the whirls together.

Note: Filled biscuits are best served on the day they are made. Unfilled biscuits will keep, stored in an airtight container, for up to 1 week, or frozen for up to 3 months.

CINNAMON CHOCOLATE SHORTBREAD

MAKES 32

200 g (7 oz/1⅔ cups) plain (all-purpose) flour
40 g (1½ oz/⅓ cup) unsweetened cocoa powder
1½ teaspoons ground cinnamon
250 g (9 oz) unsalted butter
60 g (2¼ oz/½ cup) icing (confectioners') sugar
caster (superfine) sugar, for sprinkling

1 Preheat the oven to 160°C (315°F/Gas 2–3). Line two baking trays with baking paper. Sift together the flour, cocoa and cinnamon. Using electric beaters, beat the butter and icing sugar until light and creamy. Using a large metal spoon, fold in the sifted flour mixture. Turn the dough out onto a lightly floured surface and knead gently until smooth.

2 Roll out the dough between two sheets of baking paper until 1 cm (½ inch) thick. Using a 7 cm (2 ¾ inch) star cutter, cut out the biscuits. Place on the prepared trays, leaving room for spreading. Prick the dough with a fork, sprinkle the top with the caster sugar and refrigerate for 30 minutes.

3 Bake for 15–18 minutes, swapping trays halfway through cooking. Allow to cool on the trays.

LIME AND WHITE CHOCOLATE FINGERS

MAKES 18

250 g (9 oz/2 cups) plain
  (all-purpose) flour

1 teaspoon baking powder

145 g (5 oz/⅔ cup) caster
  (superfine) sugar

75 g (2½ oz) unsalted butter, melted

2 tablespoons lime juice

grated zest from 2 limes

1 teaspoon natural vanilla extract

1 egg, lightly beaten

1 egg yolk

150 g (5½ oz/1 packed cup) white
  chocolate, chopped

1 **Preheat the oven** to 170°C (325°F/Gas 3). Lightly grease and flour two baking trays.

2 **Sift the flour** and baking powder into a large bowl and stir in the sugar. Whisk together the butter, lime juice, zest, vanilla, egg and egg yolk until combined. Add the butter mixture to the flour mixture and stir until a firm dough forms.

3 **Take tablespoonfuls** of the dough and, on a lightly floured board, roll into thin logs 12 cm (4 ½ inches) long. Place on the prepared trays and bake for 10 minutes, or until firm, swapping the position of the trays halfway through cooking. Cool on the trays for 5 minutes, then remove to a wire rack to cool completely.

4 **Put the chocolate** in a small heatproof bowl. Sit the bowl over a small saucepan of simmering water, stirring frequently until the chocolate has melted. Take care that the base of the bowl doesn't touch the water.

5 **To decorate the biscuits,** place them close together on the wire rack (put a piece of paper towel under the rack to catch the drips) and, using a fork dipped into the melted chocolate, drizzle the chocolate over the biscuits. Leave to set.

Note: These fingers will keep, stored in an airtight container, for up to 2 days. Undecorated biscuits will keep up to 7 days in an airtight container, or up to 8 weeks in the freezer.

CRACKLE COOKIES

MAKES 60

125 g (4½ oz) unsalted butter, cubed and softened

370 g (12 oz/2 cups) soft brown sugar

1 teaspoon vanilla essence

2 eggs

60 g (2 oz) dark chocolate, melted

80 ml (3 fl oz/⅓ cup) milk

340 g (11 oz/2¾ cups) plain flour

2 tablespoons cocoa powder

2 teaspoons baking powder

¼ teaspoon ground allspice

90 g (3 oz/⅔ cup) chopped pecan nuts

icing (confectioners') sugar, to coat

1 Lightly grease two baking trays. Beat the butter, sugar and vanilla until light and creamy. Beat in the eggs, one at a time. Stir the chocolate and milk into the butter mixture.

2 Sift the flour, cocoa, baking powder, allspice and a pinch of salt into the butter mixture and mix well. Stir the pecans through. Refrigerate for at least 3 hours, or overnight.

3 Preheat oven to 180°C (350°F/Gas 4). Roll tablespoons of the mixture into balls and roll each in the icing sugar to coat.

4 Place well apart on the trays. Bake for 20–25 minutes, or until lightly browned. Leave for 3–4 minutes, then cool on a wire rack.

CLASSIC SHORTBREAD

SERVES 4

225 g (8 oz) unsalted butter

115 g (4 oz/½ cup) caster (superfine)
 sugar, plus extra for dusting

225 g (8 oz/1¾ cups) plain
 (all-purpose) flour

115 g (4 oz/⅔ cup) rice flour

1 **Preheat the oven** to 190°C (375°F/Gas 5). Lightly grease two baking trays.

2 **Cream the butter** and sugar in a bowl using electric beaters until pale and fluffy. Sift in the flour, rice flour and a pinch of salt and, using a wooden spoon, stir into the creamed mixture until it resembles fine breadcrumbs. Transfer to a lightly floured work surface and knead gently to form a soft dough. Cover with plastic wrap and refrigerate for 30 minutes.

3 **Divide dough** in half and roll out one half on a lightly floured work surface to form a 20 cm (8 inch) round. Carefully transfer to a prepared tray. Using a sharp knife, score surface of the dough into eight equal wedges, prick the surface lightly with a fork and, using your fingers, press edges to form a fluted effect. Repeat this process with remaining dough to make a second round. Lightly dust shortbreads with extra sugar.

4 **Bake** for 18–20 minutes, or until the shortbreads are light golden. Remove from the oven and while still hot, follow the score marks and cut into wedges. Cool on the baking tray for 5 minutes, then transfer to a wire rack.

Note: Shortbread will keep, stored in an airtight container, for up to 1 week. Shortbread can be made with plain flour alone; however, the addition of rice flour produces a lighter result.

CHOCOLATE, RAISIN AND PEANUT CLUSTERS

MAKES ABOUT 40

200 g (7 oz) dark chocolate

60 g (2¼ oz) unsalted butter, chopped

170 g (6 oz/¾ cup) caster (superfine) sugar

1 tablespoon golden syrup or dark corn syrup

1½ teaspoons natural vanilla extract

155 g (5½ oz/1¼ cups) raisins

200 g (7 oz/1¼ cups) peanut halves, toasted and roughly chopped

40 g (1½ oz/⅓ cup) plain (all-purpose) flour

2 tablespoons unsweetened cocoa powder

---

1 **Preheat the oven** to 170°C (325°F/Gas 3). Lightly grease two baking trays.

2 **Roughly chop** 80 g (2¾ oz) of the chocolate and put in a heatproof bowl along with the butter, sugar, golden syrup and vanilla. Put the bowl over a saucepan of simmering water, stirring until the chocolate and butter have melted and the mixture is smooth. Take care that the base of the bowl doesn't touch the water. Allow to cool slightly.

3 **Roughly chop** the remaining chocolate and combine with the raisins and peanuts in a large bowl. Sift the flour and cocoa powder over the peanut mixture. Toss to combine. Add the melted chocolate mixture and, using a wooden spoon, stir until the mixture is well combined and a firm dough forms.

4 **Using a tablespoon** of the mixture at a time, form into rough rounds, then place on the trays, spacing the biscuits about 4 cm (1½ inches) apart. Bake for 15 minutes, swapping the position of the trays halfway through cooking, or until the biscuits are firm and no longer glossy. Cool on the trays for 5 minutes. Carefully remove to a wire rack to cool completely.

Note: The chocolate biscuits will keep, stored in an airtight container, for up to 1 week, or frozen for up to 8 weeks.

GINGERBREAD

MAKES ABOUT 40 (DEPENDING ON SIZE OF CUTTERS)

350 g (12 oz) plain (all-purpose) flour

2 teaspoons baking powder

2 teaspoons ground ginger

100 g (3½ oz) chilled unsalted butter, diced

175 g (6 oz/¾ cup) soft brown sugar

1 egg, beaten

115 g (4 oz/⅓ cup) dark treacle

silver balls (optional)

ICING GLAZE

1 egg white

3 teaspoons lemon juice

155 g (5½ oz/1¼ cups) icing (confectioners') sugar

ROYAL ICING

1 egg white

200 g (7 oz) icing (confectioners') sugar

1 Preheat the oven to 190°C (375°F/Gas 5). Lightly grease two baking trays.

2 Sift flour, baking powder, ground ginger and a pinch of salt into a bowl. Rub in butter until the mixture resembles fine breadcrumbs, then stir in sugar. Make a well in the centre, add egg and treacle and, using a wooden spoon, stir until a soft dough forms. Transfer to a clean surface. Knead until smooth.

3 Divide the dough in half and roll out on a lightly floured work surface until 5 mm (¼ inch) thick. Using various shaped cutters (hearts, stars or flowers), cut into desired shapes, then transfer to the prepared trays. Bake in batches for 8 minutes, or until the biscuits are light brown. Cool on the trays for 2–3 minutes, then transfer to a wire rack to cool completely. (If using the biscuits as hanging decorations, use a skewer to make a small hole in each one while still hot.

4 To make the glaze, whisk the egg white and lemon juice together until foamy, then whisk in the icing sugar to form a smooth, thin icing. Cover the surface with plastic wrap until needed.

5 To make the royal icing, lightly whisk the egg white until just foamy, then gradually whisk in enough icing sugar to form a soft icing. Cover the surface with plastic wrap until needed.

6 Brush a thin layer of glaze over some of the biscuits and leave to set. Using an icing bag (or see tip, below) filled with royal icing, decorate the biscuits as shown in the photograph, or as desired.

Note: Store the glazed gingerbread for up to 3 days in an airtight container.

WALNUT AND ORANGE BISCOTTI

MAKES ABOUT 40

250 g (9 oz/2½ cups) walnut halves, lightly toasted

310 g (11 oz/2½ cups) plain (all-purpose) flour, plus extra for rolling

1 teaspoon baking powder

½ teaspoon bicarbonate of soda (baking soda)

170 g (6 oz/¾ cup) caster (superfine) sugar

3 eggs, lightly beaten

grated zest from 3 oranges

2 teaspoons natural vanilla extract

1 Preheat the oven to 170°C (325°F/Gas 3). Lightly grease a baking tray.

2 Roughly chop the walnuts and set aside. Sift the flour, baking powder and bicarbonate of soda into a large bowl, then stir in the sugar. Combine the eggs, orange zest and vanilla in a bowl and stir with a fork to mix well. Pour egg mixture into the flour mixture and stir until nearly combined. Using your hands, knead briefly to form a firm dough. Put the dough on a lightly floured work surface and knead walnuts into the dough.

3 Divide the dough into three even-sized pieces. Working with one piece of dough at a time, roll each piece to form a 29 cm (11½ inch) log. Gently pat the surface to flatten the log to a 4 cm (1½ inch) width, then place on prepared tray and bake for 30 minutes, or until light golden and firm. Remove from the oven and allow to cool for 15 minutes.

4 Reduce the oven to 150°C (300°F/Gas 2). When the logs are cool enough to handle, remove to a board and, using a sharp, serrated knife, cut the logs on the diagonal into 1 cm (½ inch) thick slices. Arrange in a single layer on the two baking trays and bake for 15 minutes, swapping the position of the trays halfway through cooking, or until the biscotti are dry. Cool on a wire rack.

Note: Biscotti will keep, stored in an airtight container, for up to 3 weeks.

THUMBPRINT BISCUITS

MAKES ABOUT 45

250 g (9 oz) unsalted butter, softened

140 g (5 oz/1 heaped cup) icing (confectioners') sugar

1 egg yolk, lightly beaten

90 g (3¼ oz/1 ⅓ cup) cream cheese, softened and cut into chunks

1½ teaspoons natural vanilla extract

1 teaspoon finely grated lemon zest

350 g (12 oz/2¾ cups) plain (all-purpose) flour, sifted

¼ teaspoon baking powder

½ teaspoon bicarbonate of soda (baking soda)

2 tablespoons each apricot, blueberry and raspberry jam

1   Preheat the oven to 180°C (350°F/Gas 4) and grease three baking trays.

2   Cream the butter, icing sugar and egg yolk in a bowl using electric beaters until pale and fluffy, then beat in the cream cheese, vanilla and lemon zest until smooth. Combine the flour, baking powder, bicarbonate of soda and ¼ teaspoon salt in a large bowl and, using a wooden spoon, gradually stir into the creamed mixture until a soft dough forms. Set aside for 5–10 minutes, or until the dough firms up.

3   Break off small (15 g/½ oz) pieces of dough, shape into balls and flatten slightly to make 4 cm (1 ½ inch) rounds. Transfer to prepared trays and make a small indent in the centre of each with your thumb. Spoon about ¼ teaspoon of apricot jam into one-third of the biscuits, ¼ teaspoon blueberry jam into one-third, and ¼ teaspoon of raspberry jam into the remaining one-third of the biscuits. Bake for 10–12 minutes, or until light golden. Cool for a few minutes on the trays, then transfer to a wire rack.

Note: These biscuits are best eaten the same day but will keep, stored in an airtight container, for up to 2 days.

CHOCOLATE AND CINNAMON ALPHABET BISCUITS

MAKES ABOUT 32

125 g (4½ oz) unsalted butter, softened

115 g (4 oz) caster (superfine) sugar

1 egg, lightly beaten

½ teaspoon natural vanilla extract

225 g (8 oz) plain (all-purpose) flour

30 g (1 oz/¼ cup) unsweetened cocoa powder

½ teaspoon baking powder

2 teaspoons ground cinnamon

1 egg white

1 tablespoon caster (superfine) sugar, extra

1 teaspoon ground cinnamon

1 **Preheat the oven** to 190°C (375°F/Gas 5). Lightly grease two baking trays.

2 **Cream the butter** and sugar in a bowl using electric beaters until pale and fluffy, then beat in the egg and vanilla. Sift in the flour, cocoa powder, baking powder and cinnamon and, using a wooden spoon, stir into the creamed mixture until a soft dough forms. Cover the dough with plastic wrap and refrigerate for 30 minutes.

3 **Roll out dough** between two sheets of baking paper to 5 mm (¼ inch) thick. Cut out the letters using alphabet cutters.

4 **To make a glaze for the biscuits,** whisk the egg white with a fork until frothy, then set aside. Combine the extra sugar and ground cinnamon in a small bowl.

5 **Brush the tops of the biscuits** with the glaze, scatter over the cinnamon sugar and bake for 10 minutes, or until browned. Cool on the trays for 2 minutes, then transfer to a wire rack to cool completely.

Note: The biscuits will keep, stored in airtight container, for up to 1 week.

CHOCOLATE FUDGE SANDWICHES

MAKES 20–24

250 g (9 oz/2 cups) plain
(all-purpose) flour

30 g (1 oz/¼ cup) unsweetened
cocoa powder

200 g (7 oz) unsalted butter, chilled
and diced

100 g (3½ oz/heaped ¾ cup) icing
(confectioners') sugar

2 egg yolks, lightly beaten

1 teaspoon natural vanilla extract

FILLING

100 g (3½ oz/⅔ cup) chopped dark
chocolate

1 tablespoon golden syrup or dark
corn syrup

25 g (1 oz) unsalted butter, softened

1 Preheat the oven to 200°C (400°F/Gas 6). Lightly grease two baking trays.

2 Sift the flour and cocoa powder into a bowl and rub in the butter until the mixture resembles fine breadcrumbs. Sift in the icing sugar and stir to combine. Using a wooden spoon, gradually stir in the egg yolks and vanilla until a soft dough forms.

3 Transfer the dough to a lightly floured work surface and shape into a 4 x 6 x 26 cm (1 ½ x 2½ x 10½ inch) block. Wrap in plastic wrap and chill for 30 minutes, or until firm. Cut the dough into 40–48 slices, about 5 mm (¼ inch) wide. Place the slices, spacing them well apart, on the baking trays. Bake for 10 minutes, or until firm. Cool on the trays for 5 minutes, then transfer to a wire rack to cool completely.

4 To make the filling, put the chocolate in a small heatproof bowl. Sit the bowl over a small saucepan of simmering water, stirring frequently until the chocolate has melted. Take care that the base of the bowl doesn't touch the water. Remove from the heat, stir in the golden syrup and butter and continue stirring until the mixture is smooth. Allow to cool a little, then put in the refrigerator and chill for 10 minutes, or until the mixture is thick enough to spread. Use the chocolate filling to sandwich the biscuits together.

Note: Filled biscuits are best eaten on the day they are made. Unfilled biscuits will keep, stored in an airtight container, for up to 3 days.

CRANBERRY AND HAZELNUT REFRIGERATOR BISCUITS

MAKES ABOUT 50

125 g (4½ oz/1 cup) icing
(confectioners') sugar, sifted

175 g (6 oz) unsalted butter, softened

2 egg yolks

2 teaspoons lemon juice

185 g (6½ oz/1½ cups) plain
(all-purpose) flour, sifted

110 g (3¾ oz/1 cup) ground hazelnuts
(filberts)

150 g (5½ oz/1½ cups) sweetened dried
cranberries

80 g (2¾ oz/½ cup) poppy seeds

1 **Cream the icing sugar** and butter in a bowl until pale and fluffy. Add the egg yolks and lemon juice and beat to combine well. Add the flour and ground hazelnuts and stir to combine well, then stir in the cranberries. Divide the mixture in half.

2 **Scatter half the poppy seeds** over a 30 cm (12 inch) long piece of foil. Place one half of the mixture on the work surface and form into a 20 cm (8 inch) long sausage shape. Transfer the dough to the foil, firmly rolling the dough in the poppy seeds to coat, then roll tightly in the foil to form a neat cylinder, twisting the ends tight. Repeat with the remaining poppy seeds and dough and another piece of foil. Refrigerate the dough for a minimum of 4 hours, but it can be left for up to 5 days.

3 **When you are ready** to bake the biscuits, preheat the oven to 170°C (325°F/Gas 3). Lightly grease two baking trays. Remove the foil and, using a large serrated knife, cut the dough into 8 mm (3/8 inch) thick slices. Place the rounds on the baking trays and bake for 12–15 minutes, or until firm and lightly coloured. Cool on the trays for 5 minutes, then transfer to a wire rack.

Note: An uncooked log of dough can be frozen, ready to be thawed, sliced and baked, when needed. Cooked, the biscuits will keep, stored in an airtight container, for up to 1 week.

HONEY AND CARDAMOM BISCUITS

MAKES 24

200 g (7 oz) unsalted butter

150 g (5½ oz/⅔ cup) caster (superfine) sugar

3 tablespoons honey

250 g (9 oz/2 cups) plain (all-purpose) flour

1 teaspoon baking powder

80 g (2¾ oz/¾ cup) ground almonds

2 teaspoons ground cardamom

icing (confectioners') sugar, for dusting

1 Preheat the oven to 170°C (325°F/Gas 3). In a small saucepan, melt the butter, sugar and honey over medium heat, stirring until the sugar dissolves.

2 In a large bowl, sift the flour and baking powder. Stir in ground almonds and cardamom. Make a well in the centre and add the butter mixture. Stir until just combined.

3 Place tablespoons of the mixture onto baking trays lined with baking paper. Flatten slightly with the base of a glass and bake for 15–18 minutes, or until lightly golden. Rest on trays for 5 minutes before transferring to a wire rack to cool completely. Dust lightly with icing sugar.

COCONUT MACAROONS

MAKES ABOUT 64

4 egg whites, lightly beaten

450 g (1 lb/2 cups) caster (superfine) sugar

1½ tablespoons liquid glucose

1½ teaspoons natural vanilla extract

180 g (6 oz/2 cups) desiccated coconut

125 g (4½ oz/1 cup) plain (all-purpose) flour

1 **Combine the egg whites,** sugar and liquid glucose in a large heatproof bowl and whisk to combine. Place the bowl over a saucepan of simmering water and whisk until the mixture is just warm. Remove from the heat and add the vanilla, coconut and flour and stir to combine well. Cover the bowl with plastic wrap and refrigerate the mixture until firm.

2 **Meanwhile,** preheat the oven to 150°C (300°F/Gas 2). Line two baking trays with baking paper.

3 **Take a heaped teaspoonful** of the mixture and, using wet hands, form the mixture into balls. Flatten the balls slightly and place them on the trays, spacing them apart. Bake for about 15 minutes, or until macaroons are light golden. Swap the position of the trays halfway through cooking. Cool 5 minutes on the tray. Transfer to a wire rack to cool completely.

Note: Macaroons will keep, stored in an airtight container, for up to 1 week, or frozen for up to 8 weeks. Use large baking trays, if you have them, as you'll need to give the macaroons room to spread. Alternatively, cook them in two batches.

CINNAMON PECAN BISCOTTI

MAKES 30

2 eggs, at room temperature

250 g (9 oz/heaped 1 cup) caster (superfine) sugar

280 g (10 oz/2¼ cups) plain (all-purpose) flour

½ teaspoon baking powder

2 teaspoons ground cinnamon

125 g (4 oz/1¼ cups) pecans

1 **Preheat the oven** to 170°C (325°F/Gas 3). Line a baking tray with baking paper. Using electric beaters, beat the eggs and sugar for 2 minutes, or until pale and thick. Add the sifted flour, baking powder, cinnamon and pecans. Use a flat-bladed knife to mix to a soft dough. Turn out onto a lightly floured surface and knead until the mixture comes together.

2 **Divide the mixture** into two equal portions. Shape each portion into logs about 25 cm (10 inches) long and 8 cm (3 inches) wide. Place the logs on the prepared tray, leaving room for spreading, and bake for 35–40 minutes, or until lightly coloured. Set aside to cool completely.

3 **Using a serrated knife,** cut the logs into 1 cm (½ inch) thick slices and place in a single layer, cut side down, on the tray. Bake for 15–20 minutes, or until crisp and lightly golden in colour, turning halfway through cooking. Allow to cool completely on the tray.

ORANGE POLENTA BISCUITS

MAKES 20–22

125 g (4½ oz) unsalted butter, softened

80 g (2¾ oz/⅓ cup) caster (superfine) sugar

1 teaspoon orange flower water

finely grated zest from 1 orange

2 eggs, lightly beaten

165 g (5¾ oz/1⅓ cups) plain (all-purpose) flour

80 g (2¾ oz/½ cup) polenta (cornmeal)

1 **Preheat the oven** to 200°C (400°F/Gas 6). Line two baking trays with baking paper.

2 **Combine the butter,** sugar, orange flower water and orange zest in a food processor and process until light and creamy. Add the eggs and process until smooth. Add the flour and polenta and pulse until a sticky dough forms.

3 **Transfer the mixture** to a piping bag fitted with a 2 cm (¾ inch) star nozzle. Pipe mixture onto the prepared baking trays to form 7 cm (2¾ inch) crescents. Bake for 15 minutes, or until the biscuits are golden around the edges. Cool on the trays for 5 minutes. Transfer to a wire rack to cool completely.

Note: Orange polenta biscuits will keep, stored in an airtight container, for up to 3 days.

OATCAKES

MAKES 30–32

400 g (14 oz/3¼ cups) fine oatmeal

100 g (3½ oz/⅔ cup) oat bran

1 teaspoon bicarbonate of soda (baking soda)

60 g (2¼ oz) butter, melted

1 **Preheat the oven** to 200°C (400°F/Gas 6). Lightly grease two baking trays.

2 **Combine the oatmeal,** oat bran, bicarbonate of soda and 1 teaspoon salt in a bowl. Make a well in the centre and, using a wooden spoon, stir in the melted butter and 250 ml (9 fl oz/ 1 cup) water to form a firm, slightly sticky dough.

3 **Transfer the dough** to a lightly floured work surface and knead until smooth. Roll out on a floured surface to a 2 mm (1⁄16 inch) round and, using a 7 cm (2 ¾ inch) pastry cutter, cut out rounds from the dough (rerolling the pastry scraps to press out a total of 30–32 rounds).

4 **Transfer** to the baking trays and bake for 18–20 minutes, or until edges are lightly browned. Cool on trays for 5 minutes, then transfer to a wire rack to cool. Serve with cheeses, such as a blue cheese or a mature cheddar.

Note: Oatcakes will keep, stored in an airtight container, for up to 1 week.

CUMIN SEED WAFERS

MAKES 48

250 g (9 oz/2 cups) plain (all-purpose) flour
1 teaspoon baking powder
60 g (2¼ oz) Copha (white vegetable shortening), chilled
1 tablespoon cumin seeds, toasted

1 Preheat the oven to 180°C (350°F/Gas 4). Lightly grease two baking trays.

2 Sift the flour, baking powder and 1 teaspoon salt into a bowl. Rub in the Copha until the mixture resembles fine breadcrumbs. Stir in the cumin seeds. Make a well in the centre of mixture and gradually add 125 ml (4 fl oz/ ½ cup) water, stirring with a wooden spoon until a dough forms. Knead the dough gently on a lightly floured work surface until just smooth. Cover with plastic wrap and refrigerate for 30 minutes.

3 Divide the dough into quarters and roll out each quarter on a floured work surface until 1 mm (¹⁄₁₆ inch) thick, then trim the sides to form a 20 x 30 cm (8 x 12 inch) rectangle. Cut in half down the length, then cut across the width to form 5 cm (2 inch) wide fingers. You should end up with 12 fingers from each quarter of dough. Place on the baking trays and bake in batches for 10–12 minutes, or until light golden. Transfer to a wire rack to cool.

Note: These wafers will keep, stored in an airtight container, for up to 1 week. Take care when dry-roasting cumin seeds, as they can burn quite quickly. Place the seeds in a dry, heavy-based frying pan over low heat and heat just until fragrant.

PLUM AND CARAWAY BISCUITS

MAKES 24

80 g (2¾ oz) butter, softened

60 g (2¼ oz/heaped ⅓ cup) cream cheese, chopped

115 g (4 oz/½ cup) caster (superfine) sugar

1 teaspoon natural vanilla extract

2 egg yolks

1½ teaspoons caraway seeds

150 g (5½ oz/1¼ cups) plain (all-purpose) flour

plum jam

icing (confectioners') sugar, for dusting

1   Cream the butter, cream cheese and sugar in a bowl using electric beaters until pale and fluffy. Add the vanilla and 1 egg yolk and beat to combine well. Add the caraway seeds and flour and stir until a dough forms. Turn the dough out onto a lightly floured work surface, form into a flat rectangle, then cover with plastic wrap and refrigerate for 2 hours, or until firm.

2   Preheat the oven to 180°C (350°F/Gas 4). Lightly grease two baking trays. Mix remaining egg yolk with 2 teaspoons water and stir to combine thoroughly.

3   Cut the dough in half, then roll out each half on a lightly floured work surface to form an 18 x 24 cm (7 x 9 ½ inch) rectangle. Using a lightly floured sharp knife, cut the dough into 6 cm (2½ inch) squares. Place a scant teaspoon of jam diagonally across the centre of each square, then brush all four corners of the square with the egg mixture. Take one corner and fold it into the centre. Take the opposite corner and fold it into the centre, overlapping the first corner slightly, to partially enclose the jam.

4   Brush the tops of the biscuits with the egg mixture, then place them, seam side up, on the baking trays. Bake for 10–12 minutes, or until light golden, swapping the position of the trays halfway through cooking. Cool on the trays for 5 minutes, then transfer to a wire rack to cool completely. Dust with icing sugar before serving.

Note: The biscuits will keep, stored in an airtight container, for up to 1 week.

SPICED TREACLE GINGERBREADS

MAKES 36

140 g (5 oz) unsalted butter, cubed and softened
115 g (4 oz/½ cup) dark brown sugar
90 g (3¼ oz/¼ cup) treacle, preferably black
1 egg
250 g (9 oz/2 cups) plain (all-purpose) flour
30 g (1 oz/¼ cup) self-raising flour
3 teaspoons ground ginger
2 teaspoons ground cinnamon
¾ teaspoon ground cloves
¾ teaspoon ground nutmeg
1 teaspoon bicarbonate of soda

TINTED ICING

1 egg white
½ teaspoon lemon juice
125 g (4½ oz/1 cup) icing (confectioners') sugar, sifted
assorted food colourings

1 **Lightly grease** two baking trays. Beat the butter and sugar until light and creamy, then beat in the treacle and egg. Fold in the combined sifted flours, spices and bicarbonate of soda. Turn out onto a lightly floured surface and knead until smooth. Cover with plastic wrap and chill for 10 minutes.

2 **Divide the dough** in half and roll out between two sheets of lightly floured baking paper to a 4 mm thickness. Lay the dough on the trays and chill for 15 minutes until just firm. Preheat the oven to 180°C (350°F/Gas 4).

3 **Cut out** the dough using a 7 cm heart-shaped cutter. Using a 1 cm plain cutter, cut a hole at the top of each heart. (You can thread these with ribbon to hang up the biscuits.) Place on the trays and bake for 10 minutes. Leave 5 minutes, then cool on a wire rack.

4 **To make the icing,** whisk the egg white until foamy. Add the lemon juice and sugar and stir until glossy. Tint the icing any colour you want, then spoon into paper piping bags, seal the end and snip off the tip. Decorate the biscuits with the icing.

GINGER AND PISTACHIO BISCUITS

MAKES 25

100 g (3½ oz) unsalted butter

125 g (4½ oz/⅔ cup) soft brown sugar

1 teaspoon natural vanilla extract

2 eggs, at room temperature

250 g (9 oz/2 cups) plain
   (all-purpose) flour

1½ teaspoons baking powder

2 teaspoons ground ginger

100 g (3½ oz/⅔ cup) pistachio nuts,
   roughly chopped

white chocolate, for drizzling (optional)

1 Preheat the oven to 170°C (325°F/Gas 3). Line two baking trays with baking paper. Using electric beaters, beat together the butter, sugar and vanilla until light and creamy. Add the eggs, one at a time, and beat until well combined.

2 Fold through the combined sifted flour, baking powder and ginger. Stir through the pistachio nuts. Using lightly floured hands, roll tablespoons of the mixture into balls, place on the prepared trays, allowing room for spreading. Flatten the biscuits slightly with a lightly floured fork.

3 Bake for 15–18 minutes, or until crisp and golden, swapping the trays halfway through cooking. Allow to cool on the trays for 5 minutes before transferring to a wire rack to cool. Drizzle the biscuits with white chocolate, if desired.

CHOC CHIP COOKIES

MAKES 16

125 g unsalted butter

185 g (1 cup) soft brown sugar

1 teaspoon natural vanilla extract

1 egg, lightly beaten

1 tablespoon milk

215 g (1¾ cups) plain flour 1 teaspoon baking powder

250 g (1½ cups) dark chocolate bits (chocolate chips)

1 **Preheat the oven** to 180°C (350°F/Gas 4). Line a large baking tray with baking paper.

2 **Cream the butter and sugar** with electric beaters in a large bowl. Mix the vanilla essence and gradually add the egg, beating well. Stir in the milk. Sift the flour and baking powder into a large bowl, then fold into the butter and egg mixture. Stir in the dark chocolate bits.

3 **Drop level tablespoons** of the cookie mixture onto the baking tray, leaving about 4 cm (1 ½ inch) between each cookie. Lightly press with a floured fork. Bake 15 minutes, or until lightly golden. Cool on a wire rack.

SLICES

SLICES BASICS

Crunchy, gooey, sticky, fruity, spongy, fudgy, chewy, creamy, nutty, chocolatey – whatever your culinary craving, a slice can satisfy it simply and completely. The slice has long been a favourite accompaniment for morning coffee or afternoon tea. Most are quick and easy to cook and for the beginner, slices are a dream come true: less daunting to prepare than a cake, but a lot more exciting than a batch of cookies. Cut a piece as little or as large as you like and indulge yourself.

Equip yourself

We've used an assortment of tins in our recipes to suit both the flavour and richness of each slice, giving a selection of shapes, sizes and thicknesses. Don't forget: always measure your tins across the base. Obviously, we don't expect everyone to have the full array of tins in their kitchen, so if you don't have the exact size specified, use the closest you have and adjust the cooking time accordingly. If you have the choice, use a slightly larger tin — your mixture will be spread a little more thinly and so will take less time to cook. If you use a smaller tin, your mixture is likely to bubble up over the top. It may take slightly longer to cook. Using a non-stick tin means your slice will cook slightly faster and brown more — check it about 5 minutes earlier than the cooking time given in the recipe.

Basic metric cup and spoon measures and scales will help you measure your ingredients accurately and appliances such as electric beaters and food processors will help minimise preparation time.

Tin talk

Lining the tin has a dual purpose — it prevents the slice sticking to the tin but also means you can lift your slice out of the tin after cooking. Line the tin before you start any mixing. Lightly grease the base and sides with butter or oil spray, then line the base with a piece of non-stick baking paper. The paper should fit the base of the tin neatly, without creases, but should be wide so that it overhangs the two long sides of the tin. This creates the simple handles that enable you to lift your slice out of the tin. Some recipes may only require the base to be lined. To do this, draw around the base onto paper, then cut it out. If all four sides of the tin need to be lined, simply line the base, overhanging two sides, then lay another piece of paper over the top, overhanging the other two sides.

In the oven

If the top of the slice starts to over-brown while it is cooking, cover it loosely with foil or baking paper — not tightly or the slice will become soggy. For best results, cook the slice on the middle rack in the centre of the oven.

In some recipes, you'll need to check if the slice is cooked by inserting a skewer in the centre. The skewer should come out clean, without sticky crumbs on it. If it doesn't, bake the slice for a further 5 minutes and retest. This doesn't apply to all slices as many have soft fillings. With many slices, you will find they are soft when removed from the oven and then firm up a little as they cool. This is why the recipe will often state 'leave to cool in the tin for 5 minutes'.

Most slices can be stored in an airtight container, or in the fridge in warm weather, for between three and seven days.

Cutting

Use the baking paper 'handles' to lift the whole slice out of the tin. It is much easier to cut the slice into neat squares, fingers or even diamonds if you use a ruler as a guide. For clean edges, wipe the blade of the knife with a damp cloth between each cut. Use a sawing action with a serrated knife for cakey slices. If you have cut the slice in the tin, remove the corner piece with a palette knife — this makes it easier to lift out the other pieces.

GREAT TASTES BAKING

If you leave the baking paper to overhang, you can use it to lift out the cooked slice.

If you don't have a food processor, rub the butter into the flour with your fingertips.

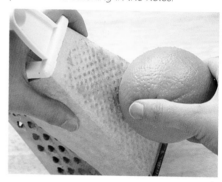
Cover the grater with baking paper to prevent rind catching in the holes.

Hints and tips

- Buy good quality, sturdy, non-stick baking tins. Always use the size of tin recommended in the recipe to ensure that cooking times stated in the recipe will work.

- Line trays or tins with baking paper so that the paper extends over the two long sides. This makes it easier to lift the cooled mixture out of the tin to cut into slices.

- If you use a food processor to make the pastry, use it only to rub the fat into the flour. After adding the liquid, pulse briefly until the mixture just comes together, then turn out onto a work surface and gently shape the dough into a ball. It is very important not to overwork the pastry dough or it will be tough when cooked.

- A soft pastry dough can be rolled out between two sheets of baking paper to prevent it from sticking to the work surface.

- If the dough is too soft to be rolled out, it may be necessary to press it into the tin. Once pressed well into the base and edges of the tin, use the back of a spoon to smooth the surface as flat and evenly as possible.

- When slices are made with several layers, it's important that each layer is completely cold before adding the next one.

- If you are short on time, a slice can be made in two stages. After lining the tin with pastry, chill it overnight, wrapped loosely in plastic wrap, ready to finish the next day.

- Slices should only be iced when cooled completely.

- Allow the cooked mixture to cool before slicing it, unless specified.

- If the cooked mixture is quite sticky and difficult to cut (eg, chocolate-topped slices), run the knife blade under hot water or dip in boiling water, then wipe dry before cutting.

- To finely grate orange or lemon rind, place a piece of baking paper over the grater. This will prevent rind getting caught in the holes.

- Toasting nuts and coconut before use enhances their flavour. Spread them out on a baking tray and toast in the oven for about 5 minutes at 180°C (350°F/Gas 4), taking care not to burn.

- Use the back of a spoon to press the slice mixture evenly into the tin.

- If you are baking 2 slices at once, swap the tins halfway through the cooking time so they brown evenly.

- Decorate slices by dusting with icing sugar or cocoa. Dust half the slice, or make decorative templates, using baking paper.

- Dip whole pieces of slice, or the corners, in melted chocolate.

- Wrap plain, un-iced pieces of slice in plastic or foil and freeze for up to 2–3 months. Pop a frozen piece into a lunchbox to thaw out by lunch time.

Some bases do not need rolling out, but can be pressed straight into the tin.

To cut chocolate-topped slices neatly, use a hot knife.

You can use uncooked rice or beans for baking blind, instead of baking beads.

DOUBLE CHOCOLATE BROWNIES

MAKES 12

80 g (2¾ oz) butter

40 g (1½ oz/⅓ cup) unsweetened cocoa powder

145 g (5 oz/⅔ cup) caster (superfine) sugar

2 eggs

60 g (2 oz/⅓ cup) plain (all-purpose) flour

½ teaspoon baking powder

90 g (3 oz/½ cup) chocolate chips

1 Preheat the oven on to 180°C (350°F/Gas 4). Grease a 20 x 30 cm (8 x 12 inch) shallow baking tin with oil or melted butter and put a piece of baking paper in the bottom.

2 Melt the butter in a saucepan. When it is ready, take it off the heat and stir in the cocoa and sugar, followed by the eggs.

3 Put a sieve over the saucepan and tip in the flour and baking powder, along with a pinch of salt. Sift everything into the saucepan, then mix it in. Make sure you don't have any pockets of flour. Add the chocolate chips and stir them in.

4 Pour the mixture into the tin and bake for 30 minutes If you have used a different-sized tin, the cooking time may be shorter (bigger tin) or longer (smaller tin). You will know your brownies are cooked when you can poke a skewer or knife into the middle of them and it comes out clean. Remember though, the chocolate chips may have melted and if your skewer hits one of those, it might look as if the mixture is still wet. Leave the slab to cool in the tin, then tip it out and cut it into brownie pieces.

GLACE FRUIT SLICE

MAKES 24

480 g (1 lb/2 cups) roughly chopped glacé fruit

2 tablespoons rum

100 g (3½ oz) unsalted butter, softened

90 g (3 oz/⅓ cup) caster (superfine) sugar

2 eggs

2 teaspoons vanilla essence

125 g (4 oz/1 cup) mixed toasted nuts, roughly chopped

30 g (1oz/¼ cup) plain flour, sifted

30 g (1 oz/¼ cup) self-raising flour, sifted

25 g (1 oz/¼ cup) milk powder

90 g (3 oz/⅔ cup) icing (confectioners') sugar

1 teaspoon rum, extra

1   **Preheat the oven** to 190°C (375°F/Gas 5). Lightly grease an 18 x 27 cm (7 x 10 ¾ inch) shallow baking tin and line with baking paper, enough to hang over the two long sides.

2   **Combine the glacé** fruit and rum in a bowl. Beat the butter and sugar with electric beaters until light and fluffy. Add the eggs one at a time, beating well after each addition. Beat in the vanilla, then stir in the fruit mixture, nuts, flours and milk powder.

3   **Spread evenly into the tin.** Bake for 15 minutes, then reduce the oven to 180°C (350°F/Gas 4) and bake for 10 minutes, or until golden brown. Cool in the tin until just warm.

4   **Combine the icing sugar,** extra rum and 1 teaspoon water until smooth and spreadable but not runny. If the icing is too thick, add a little more rum or water. Spread over the slice and cool completely. Cut into three lengthways strips, then cut each strip into eight pieces.

ORANGE AND ALMOND SLICE

MAKES 12

30 g (1 oz) rice flour

40 g (1½ oz/⅓ cup) cornflour (cornstarch)

60 g (2¼ oz/½ cup) ground almonds

2 tablespoons icing (confectioners') sugar

60 g (3 oz) unsalted butter, chopped

FILLING

1 small orange

1 egg, separated

60 g (2 oz/¼ cup) caster (superfine) sugar

80 g (2¾ oz/¾ cup) ground almonds

1 tablespoon caster (superfine) sugar, extra

LEMON ICING (FROSTING)

90 g (3¼ oz/¾ cup) icing (confectioners') sugar

1 teaspoon unsalted butter

1–1½ tablespoons lemon juice

1 **Preheat the oven** to 180°C (350°F/Gas 4). Lightly grease the base and sides of a 35 x 11 cm (14 x 4 ¼ inch) loose-based rectangular shallow tart tin.

2 **Combine the rice flour**, cornflour, almonds and icing sugar in a food processor and process briefly to just combine. Add the butter and, using the pulse button, process in short bursts just until a dough forms. Press the dough into the base of the tin, then refrigerate for 30 minutes.

3 **Meanwhile,** to make the filling, put the orange in a small saucepan with enough water to cover. Bring to the boil, then reduce the heat, cover and simmer for 30 minutes, or until soft. Drain and cool. Cut the orange in half widthways, remove any seeds, and process in a food processor until smooth.

4 **Whisk the egg yolk** and sugar in a bowl for 5 minutes, or until pale and thick, then fold in the orange purée and almonds. Using clean beaters, whisk the egg white in a clean, dry bowl until stiff peaks form. Add the extra sugar, beating until well combined, then fold into the orange mixture. Gently spread the filling over the base. Bake for 40 minutes, or until lightly browned. Cool in the tin, then remove.

5 **To make the lemon icing,** combine the sifted icing sugar and butter in a heatproof bowl with enough juice to form a thick paste. Sit the bowl over a saucepan of simmering water, stirring until the icing is smooth and runny, then remove from the heat. Working quickly, spread the icing evenly over the filling, then leave to set. Cut into 2.5 cm (1 inch) thick slices.

Note: The slice will keep, stored in an airtight container, for up to 4 days.

HONEY CARAMEL SLICE

MAKES 20

BASE

200 g (7 oz) unsalted butter, chopped

310 g (11 oz/2½ cups) plain (all-purpose) flour

115 g (4 oz/½ cup) caster (superfine) sugar

2 egg yolks, lightly beaten

FILLING

2 x 395 g (14 oz) tins sweetened condensed milk

100 g (3½ oz) unsalted butter, chopped

115 g (4 oz/⅓ cup) honey

1 Preheat the oven to 180°C (350°F/Gas 4). Lightly grease a 20 x 30 cm (8 x 12 inch) shallow tin with butter and line the base with baking paper, leaving the paper hanging over on the two long sides.

2 To make the base, combine all the ingredients, except the egg yolks, in a food processor and process until mixture resembles fine breadcrumbs. Add yolks and 1–2 tablespoons chilled water and process just until a dough forms, adding a little more water if necessary; do not overprocess. Using lightly floured hands, press half the dough over the base of the tin. Bake for 12–15 minutes, or until golden and firm to the touch. Wrap remaining dough in plastic wrap. Refrigerate until firm.

3 To make the filling, put the condensed milk and butter in a heavy-based saucepan and stir over low heat until the butter has melted. Increase the heat to medium and cook for 5–8 minutes, stirring continuously, or until the mixture has thickened. Remove from the heat and stir in the honey. Allow to cool, then pour the filling over the base and spread evenly to cover.

4 Using a grater, grate the cold dough over the caramel filling to cover, then bake for 20–30 minutes, or until golden. Cool in the tray, then carefully lift out and cut into 10 x 3 cm (4 x 1¼ inch) fingers.

Note: The honey caramel slice will keep, stored in an airtight container, for up to 3 days.

GLACE FRUIT FINGERS

MAKES 20

60 g (2¼ oz/½ cup) plain
(all-purpose) flour

2 tablespoons self-raising flour

2 tablespoons icing
(confectioners') sugar

60 g (3 oz) unsalted butter, chopped

1 egg yolk

TOPPING

350 g (12 oz) assorted light-coloured
glacé fruits (pineapple, apricots,
peaches, pears)

80 ml (2½ fl oz/⅓ cup) brandy

175 g (6 oz) unsalted butter, softened

115 g (4 oz/½ cup) caster
(superfine) sugar

2 tablespoons honey

1 egg

40 g (1½ oz/⅓ cup) plain
(all-purpose) flour

40 g (1½ oz/⅓ cup) self-raising flour

80 g (2¾ oz/½ cup) macadamia nuts,
toasted and chopped

icing (confectioners') sugar, for dusting
(optional)

1 **Preheat the oven** to 180°C (350°F/Gas 4). Lightly grease a 20 x 30 cm (8 x 12 inch) rectangular shallow tin and line the base with baking paper, leaving the paper hanging over on the two long sides.

2 **Process the flours** and icing sugar in a food processor until just combined. Add the butter and, using the pulse button, process in short bursts until the mixture is crumbly. Add the egg yolk and about 1 tablespoon water and pulse just until a dough forms. Cover with plastic wrap and refrigerate for 30 minutes.

3 **Roll out the pastry** between two sheets of baking paper until large enough to cover the base of the tin. Transfer to the tin.

4 **To make the topping,** cut the fruit into 5 mm (¼ inch) pieces with scissors or a sharp knife. Combine the fruit and brandy in a bowl, mix well and leave, covered, for about 1 hour, or until the fruit has absorbed the brandy.

5 **Cream butter,** sugar and honey in a small bowl using electric beaters until pale and fluffy. Add the egg and beat well until combined. Sift the flours together in a bowl, then stir into the creamed mixture. Stir in the glacé fruit and macadamia nuts, then spread the mixture evenly over the pastry. Bake for 30–35 minutes, or until golden brown. The topping may be slightly soft but will firm on cooling. Cool in the tin, then cut into 7.5 x 4 cm (3 x 1½ inch) pieces and dust lightly with icing sugar before serving.

Note: Glacé fruit fingers will keep, stored in an airtight container, for up to 4 days, or frozen for up to 3 months.

GREAT TASTES BAKING

RHUBARB SLICE

MAKES ABOUT 25

300 g (10 oz/2 heaped cups) rhubarb, trimmed and cut into 5 mm (¼ inch) slices

115 g (4 oz/½ cup) caster (superfine) sugar

185 g (6½ oz) unsalted butter, chopped

230 g (8 oz/1 cup) caster (superfine) sugar

½ teaspoon natural vanilla extract

3 eggs

90 g (3¼ oz/¾ cup) plain (all-purpose) flour

¾ teaspoon baking powder

1 tablespoon sugar

icing (confectioners') sugar, for dusting

1 Combine the rhubarb and sugar in a bowl and set aside, stirring occasionally, for 1 hour, or until rhubarb has released its juices and the sugar has dissolved. Strain well, discarding the liquid.

2 Preheat the oven to 180°C (350°F/Gas 4). Lightly grease a 20 x 30 cm (8 x 12 inch) shallow tin with butter. Line the base with baking paper, leaving the paper hanging over on the two long sides.

3 Cream the butter, sugar and vanilla in a bowl using electric beaters until pale and fluffy. Add the eggs one at a time, beating well after each addition. Sift the flour and baking powder over the mixture, then stir to combine.

4 Spread the mixture evenly over the base of the prepared tin, then put the rhubarb over the top in a single layer. Sprinkle with the sugar.

5 Bake for 40–45 minutes, or until golden. Leave to cool slightly in the tin, then carefully lift out and cut into squares. Dust with icing sugar and serve warm as a dessert with cream, or at room temperature as a snack.

Note: The rhubarb slice is best eaten on the day it is made.

HONEY AND ALMOND SLICE

MAKES ABOUT 30

BASE

215 g (7½ oz/1¾ cups) plain
  (all-purpose) flour

150 g (5½ oz) unsalted butter, chopped

90 g (3¼ oz/¾ cup) icing
  (confectioners') sugar

1 egg, lightly beaten

FILLING

125 g (4½ oz) unsalted butter

125 g (4½ oz) caster (superfine) sugar

2 eggs

30 g (1 oz/¼ cup) plain
  (all-purpose) flour

155 g (5½ oz/1½ cups) ground almonds

TOPPING

90 g (3¼ oz) unsalted butter, chopped

80 g (2¾ oz/⅓ cup) caster
  (superfine) sugar

1½ tablespoons honey

125 g (4½ oz/1 cup) slivered almonds

1 Preheat the oven to 180°C (350°F/Gas 4). Lightly grease a 20 x 30 cm (8 x 12 inch) tin and line the base with baking paper, leaving the paper hanging over on the two long sides.

2 To make the base, combine the flour, butter and icing sugar in a food processor and process until the mixture resembles fine breadcrumbs. Add the egg and process until a dough forms; do not overprocess. Using lightly floured hands, press the dough evenly over the base of the tin. Bake for 10 minutes, or until light golden. Cool slightly before adding the filling.

3 Meanwhile, to make the filling, cream the butter and sugar in a bowl using electric beaters until pale and fluffy. Add the eggs one at a time, beating well after each addition. Fold in the flour and ground almonds, then spread the mixture over the partly cooked base. Bake for 16–18 minutes, or until golden and firm to the touch. Set aside to cool.

4 To make the topping, put the butter, sugar, honey and almonds in a saucepan and stir over low heat until the butter melts and the sugar dissolves. Increase the heat, then boil the mixture for 3 minutes, or until it starts to come away from the side of the saucepan.

5 Working quickly and using an oiled metal spatula or palette knife, spread the mixture over the filling.

6 Bake for a further 10 minutes, or until golden brown. Cool in the tin, then lift out and cut into squares.

Note: Honey and almond slice will keep, stored in an airtight container, for up to 5 days.

GREAT TASTES BAKING

CARDAMOM PEAR SHORTCAKE

MAKES 20

250 g (9 oz) dried pears

1 tablespoon caster (superfine) sugar

275 g (9¾ oz) unsalted butter, chopped

140 g (5 oz/¾ cup) lightly packed soft brown sugar

80 g (2¾ oz/⅓ cup) caster (superfine) sugar

3 eggs

280 g (10 oz/2¼ cups) plain (all-purpose) flour

1 teaspoon baking powder

1 teaspoon ground cardamom

icing (confectioners') sugar, for dusting

1 **Preheat the oven** to 180°C (350°F/Gas 4). Lightly grease a 20 x 30 cm (8 x 12 inch) shallow tin with butter and line with baking paper, leaving paper hanging over the two long sides.

2 **Put the dried pears** in a bowl, cover with boiling water and soak for several hours, or until the pears have softened a little and the water has cooled. Drain off the water, reserving 125 ml (4 fl oz/½ cup).

3 **Put the pears** and sugar in a saucepan with the reserved soaking water. Stir to dissolve the sugar, then return to the boil and cook, covered, for 5 minutes, or until the pears are soft.

4 **Cream the butter** and sugars in a bowl using electric beaters until pale and fluffy. Add the eggs one at a time, beating well after each addition. Sift over the flour, baking powder and cardamom, then, using a large metal spoon, fold the flour mixture into the butter mixture until well combined. Spread half the mixture evenly over the base of the prepared tin. Scatter the pears over, then dot the remaining mixture over the pears to cover.

5 **Bake** for 40–45 minutes, or until golden and a skewer inserted into the centre of the cake comes out clean. Leave to cool in the tin, then carefully lift out, dust with icing sugar and cut into 10 x 3 cm (4 x 1 ¼ inch) fingers.

Note: The cardamom pear shortcake will keep, stored in an airtight container in a cool place, for up to 3 days.

CASHEW BROWNIES

MAKES 25

200 g (7 oz/1⅓ cups) dark chocolate, chopped

175 g (6 oz) unsalted butter, chopped

2 eggs

230 g (8½ oz/1 cup) soft brown sugar

40 g (1½ oz/⅓ cup) unsweetened cocoa powder

125 g (4½ oz/1 cup) plain (all-purpose) flour

80 g (2¾ oz/½ cup) unsalted cashews, toasted and chopped

100 g (3½ oz/1⅔ cup) dark chocolate, chopped, extra

ICING (FROSTING)

200 g (7 oz/1⅓ cups) dark chocolate, chopped

125 g (4½ oz/½ cup) sour cream

30 g (1 oz/¼ cup) icing (confectioners') sugar, sifted

1 Preheat the oven to 160°C (315°F/Gas 2–3). Lightly grease a 23 cm (9 inch) square shallow tin and line the base with baking paper.

2 Put the chocolate and butter in a heatproof bowl. Sit the bowl over a saucepan of simmering water, stirring frequently until the chocolate and butter have melted. Take care that the base of the bowl doesn't touch the water. Allow to cool.

3 Whisk the eggs and sugar in a large bowl for 5 minutes, or until pale and thick. Fold in the cooled chocolate mixture, then the sifted cocoa powder and flour. Fold in the cashews and extra chocolate, then pour into the tin, smoothing the top.

4 Bake for 30–35 minutes, or until brownies are just firm to the touch. (They may have a slightly soft centre when hot but will firm when cool.) Allow to cool.

5 To make the icing, put the chocolate in a small heatproof bowl. Sit the bowl over a small saucepan of simmering water, stirring frequently until the chocolate has melted. Take care that the base of the bowl doesn't touch the water. Allow to cool slightly, then add the sour cream and icing sugar and stir to mix well. Spread evenly over the cooled brownies. Leave for a few hours or overnight to firm up, then cut into squares.

Note: The brownies will keep, stored in an airtight container, for up to 5 days, or up to 3 months in the freezer.

LEMON SQUARES

MAKES 24

BASE

185 g (6½ oz/1½ cups) plain (all-purpose) flour, sifted

60 g (2¼ oz/½ cup) icing (confectioners') sugar

180 g (6 oz) unsalted butter, chopped

TOPPING

6 eggs, lightly beaten

460 g (1 lb/2 cups) caster (superfine) sugar

2 teaspoons finely grated lemon zest

250 ml (9 fl oz/1 cup) lemon juice

60 g (2¼ oz/½ cup) plain (all-purpose) flour

icing (confectioners') sugar, for dusting

1 **Preheat the oven** to 170°C (325°F/Gas 3). Lightly grease a 20 x 30 cm (8 x 12 inch) shallow tin with butter and line the base with baking paper, leaving the paper hanging over on the two long sides.

2 **To make the base,** mix the flour and icing sugar in a bowl. Using your fingertips, rub in the butter until mixture resembles breadcrumbs. Press the dough evenly over the base of the tin. Bake for 25 minutes, or until golden and firm to the touch. Set aside to cool. Reduce the oven to 160°C (315°F/Gas 2–3).

3 **To make the topping,** whisk the eggs and sugar in a bowl for 3–4 minutes, or until pale and thick. Whisk in the lemon zest and juice, then add the flour and whisk until just combined.

4 **Pour the mixture** over the base and bake for 45 minutes, or until set, covering the slice with foil for the last 20 minutes of cooking. Cool in the tin, then carefully lift out and cut into 5 cm (2 inch) squares using a hot knife. Dust with icing sugar just before serving.

Note: The lemon squares will keep, stored in an airtight container in the refrigerator, for up to 3 days.

APRICOT MERINGUE SQUARES

MAKES 24

250 g (9 oz/2 cups) plain
   (all-purpose) flour

1½ teaspoons ground cinnamon

60 g (2¼ oz/½ cup) icing
   (confectioners') sugar

200 g (7 oz) unsalted butter, chopped

APRICOT FILLING

200 g (7 oz/1 heaped cup) chopped
   dried apricots

80 g (2¾ oz/⅓ cup) caster
   (superfine) sugar

MERINGUE TOPPING

2 egg whites

80 g (2¾ oz/⅓ cup) caster
   (superfine) sugar

115 g (4 oz/1¼ cups) desiccated
   coconut

1 Preheat the oven to 180°C (350°F/Gas 4). Lightly grease a 20 x 30 cm (8 x 12 inch) shallow tin and line the base with baking paper, leaving paper hanging over the two long sides.

2 Combine the flour, cinnamon and icing sugar in a food processor and process until just combined. Add butter and, using the pulse button, pulse until the mixture is crumbly. Add 1–1½ tablespoons water and process until the mixture just forms a dough; don't overprocess. Using the back of a spoon, press the dough evenly into the prepared tin and refrigerate for 20 minutes.

3 Bake the dough for 15–20 minutes, or until golden. Remove from the oven and allow to cool.

4 Meanwhile, to make the apricot filling, combine apricots, sugar and 250 ml (9 fl oz/1 cup) water in a small saucepan. Stir over medium heat until the sugar has dissolved, then reduce the heat and simmer for 12 minutes, or until the mixture is thick. Remove from the heat and cool, then spread over the cooled base.

5 To make the topping, whisk the egg whites in a clean, dry bowl until soft peaks form. Gradually add the sugar, whisking well after each addition. Whisk until the mixture is stiff and glossy and the sugar has dissolved. Fold in the coconut. Spread the topping evenly over the filling. Bake for 15 minutes, or until the topping is just firm to touch. Cool completely before cutting into 5 x 5 cm (2 x 2 inch) squares.

Note: The apricot meringue squares will keep, stored in an airtight container, for up to 4 days.

MAKES 25

BASE

125 g (4½ oz) unsalted butter, chopped

70 g (2½ oz/½ cup) icing (confectioners') sugar, plus extra for dusting

185 g (6½ oz/1½ cups) plain (all-purpose) flour, sifted

TOPPING

250 ml (9 fl oz/1 cup) milk

30 g (1 oz) unsalted butter

150 g (5½ oz) soft goat's cheese, crumbled

100 g (3½ oz) cream cheese, chopped

1 teaspoon finely grated lemon zest

60 ml (2 fl oz/¼ cup) lemon juice

2 tablespoons caster (superfine) sugar

30 g (1 oz/¼ cup) cornflour (cornstarch)

60 g (2¼ oz/½ cup) sultanas (golden raisins), chopped

3 egg whites

80 g (2¾ oz/⅓ cup) caster (superfine) sugar, extra

1 **Preheat the oven** to 180°C (350°F/Gas 4). Lightly grease a 20 x 30 cm (8 x 12 inch) shallow tin with butter and line the base with baking paper, leaving the paper hanging over on the two long sides.

2 **To make the base,** cream the butter and icing sugar in a bowl until pale and fluffy. Add the flour and stir until a dough forms. Using lightly floured hands, press the dough evenly over the base of the tin. Bake for 15-20 minutes, or until golden and firm to the touch. Cool.

3 **To make the topping,** combine the milk, butter, cheeses, lemon zest, lemon juice and sugar in a large saucepan and stir over medium heat for 5 minutes, or until the butter and cheeses have melted and the mixture is smooth. Combine the cornflour and 60 ml (2 fl oz/¼ cup) cold water in a small bowl and stir until smooth. Add to the cheese mixture, then, whisking continuously, bring to the boil and cook, stirring, for

3-4 minutes, or until thickened. Remove from the heat and stir in the sultanas. Set aside.

4 **Whisk the egg whites** in a clean, dry bowl until stiff peaks form. Add the sugar gradually, whisking well after each addition. Whisk until the mixture is stiff and glossy and the sugar has dissolved. Carefully fold the egg whites into the cheese mixture and mix until just combined. Spread the mixture over the cooled base.

5 **Bake 25-30 minutes,** or until firm to the touch and golden brown. Cool completely in the tin, then carefully lift out and, using a hot knife, cut into diamonds. Dust the diamonds with icing sugar to serve.

Note: The cheese slice is best served on the day it is made. For best results use freshly squeezed lemon juice and not ready-made squeezed lemon juice available in bottles.

DATE AND CINNAMON SQUARES

MAKES 36

600 g (1 lb 5 oz/3⅓ cups) pitted whole
  dried dates, chopped

1 teaspoon bicarbonate of soda
  (baking soda)

125 g (4½ oz) unsalted butter, chopped

155 g (5½ oz/⅔ cup) soft brown sugar

2 eggs

125 g (4½ oz/1 cup) plain (all-purpose)
  flour

60 g (2¼ oz/½ cup) self-raising flour

½ teaspoon ground cinnamon, plus
  ½ teaspoon, extra

60 g (2¼ oz/½ cup) icing
  (confectioners') sugar

1 Preheat the oven to 180°C (350°F/Gas 4). Lightly grease a 23 cm (9 inch) square shallow tin and line the base with baking paper.

2 Combine the dates and 500 ml (17 fl oz/2 cups) water in a medium saucepan, bring to the boil, then remove from the heat. Stir in the bicarbonate of soda and mix well. Cool to room temperature.

3 Cream the butter and sugar in a large bowl using electric beaters until pale and fluffy. Add the eggs one at a time, beating well after each addition.

4 Sift the flours and cinnamon into a bowl, then fold into the butter mixture alternately with the date mixture. Spread into the prepared tin.

5 Bake for 50 minutes, or until a skewer inserted in the centre comes out clean. Cool in the tin for 5 minutes, then turn out onto a wire rack to cool completely.

6 Cut into 36 pieces and place on a sheet of greaseproof paper. Sift the combined icing sugar and extra cinnamon over the cubes and toss to coat. Serve immediately (the coating will be absorbed into the cakes quite quickly if left to stand).

Note: Date and cinnamon squares will keep (do not coat with the icing sugar if you intend to store them), stored in an airtight container, for up to 4 days, or up to 3 months in the freezer.

SPICED CHEESECAKE SLICE

MAKES 10

250 g (9 oz) wheatmeal biscuits (cookies)

½ teaspoon ground cinnamon, plus 1 teaspoon extra

½ teaspoon ground nutmeg

100 g (3½ oz) unsalted butter, melted

500 g (1 lb 2 oz) cream cheese, at room temperature

4 tablespoons honey

3 eggs, at room temperature

85 g (3 oz/⅔ cup) sultanas (golden raisins)

1 teaspoon ground cinnamon, extra

1 Brush a 27 x 17 cm (10 ¾ x 6½ inch) shallow tin with melted butter and line base and two long sides with baking paper. Put the biscuits in a food processor with the cinnamon and nutmeg and process into crumbs. Add the butter and process until well combined. Press firmly into prepared tin and refrigerate until firm. Preheat the oven to 170°C (325°F/Gas 3).

2 Using electric beaters, beat the cream cheese and honey together until the mixture is creamy. Add the eggs one at a time, beating well after each addition. Stir through the sultanas. Pour the mixture over the base. Sprinkle over the extra cinnamon, and swirl gently with a thick bamboo skewer to create a swirled effect on the top.

3 Bake for 30–35 minutes, or until just set. Cool in the tin, then cut into pieces to serve.

SEMOLINA SYRUP SLICE

MAKES 25

55 g (2 oz/½ cup) ground almonds

170 g (6 oz/⅔ cup) plain yoghurt

230 g (8 oz/1 cup) caster (superfine) sugar

125 g (4½ oz) unsalted butter, melted

½ teaspoon natural vanilla extract

2 eggs, lightly beaten

185 g (6½ oz/1½ cups) semolina

1 teaspoon baking powder

2 tablespoons whole unsalted pistachio nuts, for decoration

SYRUP

170 g (6 oz/¾ cup) caster (superfine) sugar

1 teaspoon finely grated lemon zest

1 tablespoon lemon juice

1 **Preheat the oven** to 180°C (350°F/Gas 4). Lightly grease a 23 cm (9 inch) square shallow tin and line the base with baking paper.

2 **To make the syrup,** combine the sugar, lemon zest and lemon juice in a saucepan with 125 ml (4 fl oz/ ½ cup) water. Stir over low heat until the sugar has dissolved. Increase the heat, bring the mixture to the boil and simmer for 10 minutes without stirring. Allow to cool, then strain.

3 **Put the ground almonds** in a small frying pan and stir over medium heat for 3–5 minutes, or until lightly browned, then remove from the heat and cool.

4 **Combine the yoghurt** and sugar in a bowl, stir until well combined, then stir in the butter, vanilla and eggs. Combine the semolina and baking powder in a bowl, stir to mix well, then stir into the yoghurt mixture. Stir in almonds. Spread the mixture over the base of the tin, smoothing the surface. Arrange the pistachios evenly over the top.

5 **Bake for 35 minutes,** or until the top is lightly browned and a skewer inserted in the centre comes out clean. Pour the cold syrup over the hot slice. Leave to cool completely in the tin before cutting into squares.

Note: The slice will keep, stored in an airtight container, for up to 3 days.

APRICOT AND MACAROON SLICE

MAKES 16

100 g unsalted butter, softened

90 g (3¼ oz/⅓ cup) caster (superfine) sugar

1 egg

185 g (6½ oz/1½ cups) plain (all-purpose) flour

½ teaspoon baking powder

FILLING

250 g (9 oz/1⅓ cups) dried apricots, roughly chopped

1 tablespoon orange-flavoured liqueur, such as Grand Marnier

2 tablespoons caster (superfine) sugar

TOPPING

100 g (3½ oz) unsalted butter

90 g (3¼ oz/⅓ cup) caster (superfine) sugar

1 teaspoon natural vanilla extract

2 eggs

270 g (9½ oz/3 cups) desiccated coconut

40 g (1½ oz/⅓ cup) plain (all-purpose) flour

½ teaspoon baking powder

1 Preheat the oven to 180°C (350°F/Gas 4). Lightly grease a 20 x 30 cm (8 inch x 12 inch) baking tin and line with baking paper. Cream butter and sugar until light and fluffy. Add egg and beat well. Sift the flour and baking powder and fold into the butter mixture with a metal spoon. Press firmly into the tin and bake for 20–25 minutes, or until golden brown. Cool.

2 To make the filling, combine the apricots, orange liqueur, sugar and 125 ml (4 fl oz/ ½ cup) boiling water in a bowl and set aside for 30 minutes. Purée in a food processor. Spread evenly over the cooled base.

3 To make the topping, cream the butter, sugar and vanilla until light and fluffy. Gradually add the eggs, beating well after each addition. Fold in the coconut, flour and baking powder with a large metal spoon. Spoon onto the apricot leaving the mixture lumpy and loose — do not press down.

4 Bake for 20–25 minutes, or until lightly golden.

VANILLA SLICE

MAKES 9

500 g (1 lb 2 oz) ready-made puff pastry

250 g (9 oz/1 cup) caster (superfine) sugar

90 g (3¼ oz/¾ cup) cornflour (cornstarch)

60 g (2¼ oz/½ cup) custard powder

1 litre (35 fl oz/4 cups) cream

60 g (2¼ oz) unsalted butter, cubed

2 teaspoons natural vanilla extract

3 egg yolks

ICING (FROSTING)

185 g (6½ oz/1½ cups) icing (confectioners') sugar

60 g (2¼ oz/¼ cup) passionfruit pulp

15 g (½ oz) unsalted butter, melted

1   Preheat the oven to 210°C (415°F/Gas 6–7). Lightly grease two baking trays with oil. Line the base and sides of a shallow 23 cm square cake tin with foil, leaving the foil hanging over two opposite sides.

2   Divide the pastry in half, roll each piece to a 25 cm (10 in) square 3 mm (⅛ in) thick and put on a baking tray. Prick all over with a fork and bake for 8 minutes, or until golden. Trim each pastry sheet to a 23 cm (10 in) square. Put one sheet top-side-down in the cake tin.

3   Combine the sugar, cornflour and custard powder in a saucepan. Add the cream, stirring constantly over medium heat for 2 minutes, or until it boils and thickens. Add the butter and vanilla and stir until smooth. Remove from the heat and whisk in the egg yolks until combined. Spread the custard over the pastry in the tin, then cover with the other pastry sheet, top side down. Cool completely.

4   To make the icing, combine the icing sugar, passionfruit pulp and butter in a bowl, and stir until smooth.

5   Lift the slice out of the tin using the foil as handles. Ice the top and leave to set before cutting with a serrated knife.

STICKY TOFFEE SLICE

MAKES 18

250 g (9 oz/1⅓ cups) pitted dates, roughly chopped

1 teaspoon bicarbonate of soda (baking soda)

215 g (7½ oz) unsalted butter

185 g (6½ oz/1½ cups) self-raising flour

1 teaspoon natural vanilla extract

1 teaspoon baking powder

3 eggs

90 ml (3 fl oz/⅓ cup) milk

2 tablespoons soft brown sugar

90 g (3¼ oz/¾ cup) icing (confectioners') sugar

90 g (3¼ oz/¾ cup) chopped walnuts

1 Preheat the oven to 180°C (350°F/Gas 4). Lightly grease a 20 x 30 cm (8 in x 12in) baking tin and line with baking paper, leaving it hanging over the two long sides.

2 Place dates in a saucepan with 200 ml (7 fl oz/ ¾ cup) water, bring to the boil, then reduce the heat and simmer gently for 10 minutes — make sure that the water doesn't evaporate completely. Add the bicarbonate of soda and leave to cool.

3 Place 185 g (6½ oz) of the butter, the flour, vanilla extract, baking powder, eggs and 75 ml (2 ¼ fl oz/⅓ cup) of the milk in a food processor and mix in short bursts for 1 minute, or until well blended. Add the dates and pulse to blend. Do not overprocess the mixture.

4 Place the mixture in the tin and bake for 20 minutes, or until a skewer inserted in the centre comes out clean. Set aside to cool.

5 Place the remaining butter and milk and the brown sugar in a pan and heat gently to dissolve the sugar. Add the icing sugar and mix well. Spread over the cooled slice and sprinkle with the walnuts.

CHOCOLATE CARAMEL SLICE

MAKES 24

200 g (7 oz) plain chocolate biscuits
(cookies), crushed

100 g (3½ oz) unsalted butter, melted

2 tablespoons desiccated coconut

125 g (4½ oz) unsalted butter, extra

400 ml (14 fl oz) tin sweetened
condensed milk

90 g (3¼ oz/⅓ cup) caster
(superfine) sugar

3 tablespoons maple syrup

250 g (9 oz/1⅔ cups) dark chocolate

2 teaspoons oil

1 **Grease** a 30 x 20 cm (12in x 8in) shallow baking tin. Line with baking paper, leaving it hanging over the two long sides.

2 **Combine the biscuits,** melted butter and coconut in a bowl, then press into the tin and smooth the surface.

3 **Combine the butter,** condensed milk, sugar and maple syrup in a small saucepan. Stir over low heat for 15 minutes, or until the sugar has dissolved and the mixture is smooth, thick and lightly coloured. Remove from the heat and cool slightly. Pour over the biscuit base and smooth the surface. Refrigerate for 30 minutes, or until firm.

4 **Chop the chocolate** into small even-sized pieces and place in a heatproof bowl. Bring a saucepan of water to the boil and remove from the heat. Sit the bowl over the saucepan, making sure the bowl doesn't touch the water. Allow to stand, stirring occasionally, until the chocolate has melted. Add the oil and stir until smooth. Spread over the caramel and leave until partially set before marking into 24 triangles. Refrigerate until firm. Cut into triangles before serving.

RASPBERRY AND COCONUT SLICE

MAKES 30

280 g (10 oz/2¼ cups) plain (all-purpose) flour

3 tablespoons ground almonds

500 g (1 lb 2 oz/2 cups) caster (superfine) sugar

250 g (9 oz) unsalted butter, chilled

½ teaspoon ground nutmeg

½ teaspoon baking powder

4 eggs

1 teaspoon natural vanilla extract

1 tablespoon lemon juice

300 g (10½ oz/2½ cups) fresh or thawed frozen raspberries

90 g (3¼ oz/1 cup) desiccated coconut

icing (confectioners') sugar, to dust

1 Preheat the oven to 180°C (350°F/Gas 4). Lightly grease a 20 x 30 cm (8 in x 12 in) shallow tin and line with baking paper, leaving it hanging over the two long sides.

2 Sift 220 g (7¾ oz/1¾ cups) of the flour into a bowl. Add the ground almonds and 125 g (4½ oz/½ cup) of the caster sugar and stir to combine. Rub the butter into the flour with your fingertips until it resembles fine breadcrumbs. Press the mixture into the tin and bake for 20–25 minutes, or until golden. Reduce the oven to 150°C (300°F/Gas 2).

3 Sift the nutmeg, baking powder and the remaining flour onto a piece of baking paper. Beat the eggs, vanilla and remaining sugar with electric beaters for 4 minutes, or until light and fluffy. Fold in the flour with a large metal spoon. Stir in the lemon juice, raspberries and coconut and pour over the base.

4 Bake for 1 hour, or until golden and firm. Chill in the tin, then cut into pieces. Dust with icing sugar.

POPPY SEED SLICE

MAKES 14

135 g (4¾ oz/1 cup) plain
(all-purpose) flour

75 g (2½ oz) unsalted butter, chilled and
chopped

60 g (2¼ oz/¼ cup) caster
(superfine) sugar

1 egg yolk

40 g (1½ oz/¼ cup) poppy seeds

2 tablespoons milk, warmed

125 g (4½ oz) unsalted butter, extra

90 g (3¼ oz/⅓ cup) caster (superfine)
sugar, extra

1 teaspoon finely grated lemon zest

1 egg

90 g (3¼ oz/¾ cup) plain (all-purpose)
flour, extra, sifted

125 g (4½ oz/1 cup) icing
(confectioners') sugar

½ teaspoon finely grated lemon zest,
extra

1 tablespoon lemon juice

1 **Preheat the oven** to 180°C (350°F/Gas 4). Grease an 11 cm x 35 cm (4¼ in x 14 in) loose-based flan tin. Sift the flour into a bowl and rub in the butter with your fingers until it resembles breadcrumbs. Stir in the sugar. Make a well in the centre and add 2–3 teaspoons water and the egg yolk. Mix with a flat-bladed knife, using a cutting action until it comes together in beads. Press into a ball and flatten slightly. Cover in plastic wrap and chill for 15 minutes.

2 **Roll out the dough** to fit the base and sides of the tin. Trim the edges. Blind bake the pastry for 10 minutes then remove the paper and beads and bake for 5 minutes, or until the pastry is dry. Cool.

3 **Soak the poppy** seeds in the milk for 10 minutes. Beat the extra butter and sugar and the zest until light and fluffy. Beat in the egg and stir in the poppy seed mixture and extra flour. Spread over the pastry and bake for 25 minutes, or until light brown and cooked through. Cool in the tin until just warm.

4 **Combine the icing sugar**, extra zest and enough juice to form a paste. Spread over the slice and cool.

GREAT TASTES BAKING

GINGER CRUNCH SLICE

MAKES 16

125 g (4½ oz) unsalted butter, softened, chopped

115 g (4 oz/½ cup) caster (superfine) sugar

1 teaspoon natural vanilla extract

165 g (5¾ oz/1⅓ cups) plain (all-purpose) flour

2 teaspoons ground ginger

1 teaspoon baking powder

GINGER ICING (FROSTING)

50 g (1¾ oz) unsalted butter

1½ tablespoons golden or dark corn syrup

2 teaspoons ground ginger

90 g (3¼ oz/¾ cup) icing (confectioners') sugar

3 tablespoons chopped crystallized ginger

1 **Preheat the oven** to 180°C (350°F/Gas 4). Line the base and two long sides of a 27 x 18 cm (10 ¾ x 7 inch) shallow tin with baking paper.

2 **Put the chopped butter,** sugar and vanilla in a bowl and beat with electric beaters until creamy. Sift together the combined plain flour, ginger and baking powder. Use a metal spoon to stir in the flour mixture in two batches until it is well incorporated.

3 **Use your fingers** to press firmly and evenly into the prepared tin. Bake for 20 minutes, or until pale golden and firm to the touch.

4 **Meanwhile,** to make the ginger icing, put the butter, golden syrup, ginger, and icing sugar in a small saucepan. Stir over low heat until smooth. Pour and spread the icing evenly over the slice while the slice is hot. Mark into 16 slices and scatter over the crystallized ginger. Set aside to cool, then cut, using marks as a guide.

Note: This slice will keep refrigerated in an airtight container for up to 8 days.

CAKES

CAKES BASICS

Cake-making is a symbol of celebration – we bake them for parties, weddings, birthdays and religious festivals. They're a symbol of everyday celebration, too, as we take time out to enjoy them with a coffee or when friends drop by. Home-baked cakes come in a myriad of shapes, sizes, textures and flavours and we love them for their comfort factor.

Preparing tins

For some cakes, greasing and flouring the tin is sufficient to prevent the batter sticking to the tin, and for the cake to easily turn out of it once cooked. Use melted, unsalted butter to grease tins, unless the recipe suggests otherwise. Some cakes benefit from having a baking paper lining on the base (and, sometimes, the sides) of the tin.

LINING A ROUND CAKE TIN: Put the tin on a sheet of baking paper and trace around the base with a pencil. Cut out the marked shape. Grease the inside of the tin and position the piece of baking paper in the base.

LINING A LOAF OR RECTANGULAR CAKE TIN: Grease the inside of the tin. Put the tin in the centre of a piece of baking paper. Make a diagonal cut from each corner of the paper to the corners of the tin. Fold the paper between the cut edges to make it easier to put into the tin. Insert the paper in the greased tin, overlapping the corners of the paper, and press to secure.

Making the batter

CREAMING METHOD: Using an electric mixer, cream the butter and sugar together in a bowl until the mixture is pale and fluffy. Gradually beat in the eggs a little at a time, until incorporated. The butter and sugar are creamed sufficiently when a spoonful of mixture drops easily from the spoon when tapped gently. The flour and liquid are then added, sometimes in alternate batches. Transfer the batter to the prepared tin and smooth the top. Bake the cake as directed.

WHISKING METHOD: Put the eggs and the sugar into a bowl and, using a balloon whisk or electric hand mixer, whisk for 5–8 minutes, or until the mixture is pale, has trebled in volume and reaches the ribbon stage (the batter will leave a thick trail when the beaters are lifted). Sift over the flour and carefully fold into the batter using a large metal spoon. Stir in melted butter, if using, and transfer to the prepared tin. Bake as directed.

MELT-AND-MIX METHOD: Put the butter, sugar and any liquid into a saucepan and heat gently until the butter has melted and the ingredients are combined. Allow to cool slightly. Fold the dry ingredients together and then stir in the melted mixture, along with any eggs, until evenly combined. Pour the batter into the prepared tin. Bake as directed.

Baking the cake

Bake the cake on the centre shelf of the oven (unless otherwise directed) and cook for the amount of time specified. If two times are given, for example between 30 and 35 minutes, always check after 30 minutes.

TESTING FOR DONENESS: A cake is cooked when it starts to shrink back slightly from the edge of the tin. Or, it can be tested with a cake tester or a metal skewer. Insert the skewer in the centre of the cake and remove it — it should be totally clean. If there is any sticky cake mixture left on the skewer, return the cake to the oven and bake for a further 5 minutes before retesting. This process can be repeated until the skewer comes out clean.

TURNING OUT: After cooking, most cakes need to be turned out of their tins. Most recipes suggest that the cake is left to cool slightly in the tin, usually for about 5 minutes. After this time the cake will have firmed up sufficiently and there won't be the risk of it cracking when turned out. Run a flat-bladed knife or palette knife gently around the edge of the cake, invert it onto a wire rack, remove the tin and carefully peel away the baking paper (if using). Leave to cool completely.

TO LINE ROUND TINS: Place the tin base on a square of baking paper and trace around it. Cut the base out as marked. Cut a strip of baking paper the same length as the circumference of the tin and about 3 cm deeper than the height. Fold down a cuff about 2 cm (1 inch) deep on one edge of the strip. Cut the folded cuff diagonally at 2 cm (1 inch) intervals. Grease the tin with melted butter or oil, applying with a pastry brush. Place the strip in the tin with the folded side on the base, press the paper into the base and side of the tin. Place the round of greaseproof paper on the base, then grease the base and side of the paper lining.

Leave the cake in its tin for the specified time before turning onto a wire rack to cool.

Brush loose crumbs off the cake with a pastry brush for a smooth finish.

Feather cake by drawing the point of a skewer from centre circle to outer edge.

Hints and tips

- Before you start baking, read the recipe thoroughly and check that you have the correct quantity of ingredients and the necessary equipment.

- Bring chilled ingredients, such as butter and eggs, to room temperature.

- Always use the shape and size of tin specified in each recipe, so as to ensure cooking times are accurate. Line the tin(s) as specified in the recipe, or grease them or dust with flour.

- Position a shelf in the centre of the oven, ensuring that there is enough room above it to allow space for the cake to rise. Preheat the oven to the required temperature.

- Always weigh and measure ingredients accurately, either with scales or cup measures (although cup measures are never as accurate as weighing).

- If melting ingredients in a saucepan, never allow the mixture to boil unless specified in the recipe.

- Eggs or egg yolks should always be added to a creamed cake mixture one at a time, beating well after each addition.

- If the creamed mixture looks like it may be starting to curdle, sift in a little of the flour alternately with each egg to prevent this.

- When whisking egg whites, ensure the bowl and beaters (or whisk) are clean and dry before you start, or the egg whites won't whisk properly. The egg whites should be at room temperature.

- A raising agent should always be sifted into the bowl with the flour so that it is evenly dispersed.

- Dry ingredients should always be folded into a whisked egg and sugar mixture with a large metal spoon. Fold lightly and gently from the centre of the bowl outwards, turning the bowl a little with each fold. Fold whisked egg whites into the other ingredients (not the other way round), so as to retain as much aeration as possible.

- Spoon thick cake batters into a tin. Gently pour thinner batters. If necessary, smooth the surface of the batter using a spatula to ensure there is even cooking and browning.

- Never open the oven door during the first half of cooking time. After the halfway point, if you do need to open the door, open and close it gently.

- If the cooked cake is stuck to the cake tin, run a palette knife gently between the cake and tin before unmoulding.

- Allow the cake to cool a little before inverting it onto a wire rack to cool. So the wire rack does not mark the top of the cake, place another wire rack on the base of the cake and invert the cake onto the second rack so it is then right side up.

- If you intend to ice the cake, allow it to cool completely first, or the icing will run off. If you intend to drizzle it with hot syrup, however, do this while the cake is still hot.

Scoop nuts into the side of your hand and gently press them onto the side of the cake.

Mark midpoint around the cake with toothpicks; slice with a sharp, serrated knife.

Place strips of baking paper in a pattern. Dust with sifted icing sugar.

BASICS

EASY SPONGE CAKE WITH STRAWBERRIES AND CREAM

SERVES 6

30 g (1 oz) butter, melted

60 g (2¼ oz/½ cup) plain (all-purpose) flour

60 g (2¼ oz/½ cup) cornflour (cornstarch)

2 teaspoons cream of tartar

1 teaspoon bicarbonate of soda (baking soda)

4 eggs

170 g (6 oz/¾ cup) caster (superfine) sugar

2 tablespoons hot milk

300 ml (10½ fl oz) cream, for whipping

1 tablespoon icing (confectioners') sugar, plus extra for dusting

2 tablespoons strawberry jam

500 g (1 lb 2 oz/3⅓ cups) strawberries, hulled and sliced in half

1 **Preheat the oven** to 180°C (350°F/Gas 4). Grease two 20 cm (8 inch) round cake tins with the melted butter and line the bases with baking paper. Dust the sides of the tins with a little flour, shaking out any excess.

2 **Sift the flour,** cornflour, cream of tartar and bicarbonate of soda into a bowl, then repeat the sifting twice more.

3 **Whisk the eggs** and sugar in a large bowl for 5 minutes, or until pale and thick. Using a large metal spoon, carefully fold in the sifted flour mixture and the hot milk until they are just incorporated; take care not to overmix. Divide the mixture evenly between the two tins, then bake for 18–20 minutes, or until the cakes are golden and have shrunk slightly from the side of the tins. Leave in the tins for 5 minutes, then turn out onto a wire rack to cool.

4 **Combine the cream** and icing sugar in a bowl, then whip until soft peaks form. Place one sponge cake on a serving plate and spread with jam. Top with half the cream and half of the sliced strawberries. Cover with the second sponge cake. Spread the remaining cream over the top and top with the remaining strawberries. Dust with icing sugar and serve immediately.

Note: Sponge cake is best eaten on the day it is made. Unfilled sponges will freeze well for up to 1 month, wrapped loosely in plastic wrap.

GREAT TASTES BAKING

CHOCOLATE HAZELNUT CAKE

SERVES 6–8

200 g (7 oz/1½ cups) roasted skinned hazelnuts

200 g (7 oz/1⅓ cups) chopped good-quality dark chocolate

2 teaspoons espresso instant coffee granules

100 g (3½ oz/¾ cup) cornflour (cornstarch)

200 g (7 oz) unsalted butter, softened

185 g (6½ oz/¾ cup) raw or golden caster (superfine) sugar

4 eggs, separated

2 teaspoons hazelnut liqueur or coffee liqueur

icing (confectioners') sugar, to serve

cocoa flakes, optional, to serve

crème fraîche or vanilla ice cream, to serve

1 Preheat the oven to 170°C (325°F/Gas 3) and grease a 20 cm (8 inch) spring-form cake tin.

2 Put the hazelnuts and chocolate in a small processor fitted with the metal blade and whizz in 5-second bursts until finely chopped. Add the coffee granules and cornflour and whizz briefly to combine. Transfer to a small bowl and set aside.

3 Change the blade on the processor to the plastic blade. Add the butter and sugar and whizz in 3-second bursts until pale. Add one-quarter of the chocolate mixture, whizz in short bursts to combine, then add 1 egg yolk and whizz in short bursts to mix through. Continue in this way until all the chocolate mixture and egg yolks have been added. Add the liqueur and whizz in short bursts to combine. Transfer the mixture to a bowl.

4 Whisk the egg whites until soft peaks form. Using a metal spoon, fold a large scoop of egg whites into the chocolate mixture. Gently fold in the remaining egg whites. Spoon into the prepared tin, level the surface and bake for 30 minutes. Cover loosely with foil and bake for a further 30–35 minutes, or until a skewer inserted in the centre of the cake comes out clean. The surface of the cake will probably crack.

5 Serve the cake warm or at room temperature. Dust the surface with icing sugar and sprinkle with the cocoa flakes, if using. Cut the cake into slices; the texture will be quite moist. Serve with a scoop of crème fraîche or soft vanilla ice cream.

PINEAPPLE PECAN CAKE

SERVES 4

80 g (2¾ oz) unsalted butter, softened

250 g (9 oz/1 cup) sugar

2 eggs, lightly beaten

185 g (6½ oz/1½ cups) plain (all-purpose) flour

1¾ teaspoons baking powder

40 g (1½ oz/⅓ cup) finely chopped pecans, toasted

180 g (¾ cup) finely chopped glacé pineapple

170 ml (5½ fl oz/⅔ cup) milk

icing (confectioners') sugar, to dust

1 **Preheat the oven** to 180°C (350°F/Gas 4). Grease a 23 cm round cake tin and line the base with baking paper. Beat the butter and sugar with electric beaters until combined. Add the egg and beat until pale and creamy.

2 **Sift together** the flour, baking powder and ¼ teaspoon salt. Add to the butter mixture with the pecans, pineapple and milk, then beat on low for 1 minute, or until almost smooth.

3 **Spoon the mixture** evenly into the prepared tin and smooth the surface. Bake for 1 hour, or until a skewer comes out clean when inserted into the centre of the cake. Leave in the tin for 10 minutes before turning onto a wire rack to cool. If desired, dust with icing sugar just before serving.

Note: Glacé pineapple is available from health food stores.

GINGER FRUIT LOAF

MAKES 1 LOAF

375 g (13 oz) mixed dried fruit

160 g (5¾ oz/1 cup) chopped pitted dried dates

75 g (2½ oz/⅓ cup) glacé ginger, chopped

60 g (2¼ oz) unsalted butter, chopped

185 g (6½ oz/1 cup) soft brown sugar

1 tablespoon golden or dark corn syrup

1 teaspoon natural vanilla extract

2 eggs, lightly beaten

185 g (6½ oz/1½ cups) plain (all-purpose) flour

1 teaspoon baking powder

2 teaspoons ground ginger

1 teaspoon ground nutmeg

20 blanched almonds

1 **Put mixed fruit,** dates, glacé ginger, butter, brown sugar, golden syrup, vanilla extract and 310 ml (10 ¾ fl oz/1¼ cups) water in a saucepan. Bring slowly to the boil, then simmer over low heat for 5 minutes. Set aside to cool.

2 **Preheat the oven** to 160°C (315°F/Gas 2–3). Grease the base and sides of a 25 x 11 cm (10 x 4 ¼ inch) loaf (bar) tin and line the base with baking paper.

3 **Stir the beaten eggs** into the cooled fruit mixture. Sift together the flour, baking powder and spices. Stir the flour mixture into the fruit mixture and mix until smooth.

4 **Spoon into the prepared tin** and smooth the surface. Arrange the almonds over the surface. Bake for 1 hour 20 minutes, or until a skewer inserted in the centre comes out clean. Cover with foil if the surface and almonds are browning too much. Leave to cool in the tin for 10 minutes, then turn onto a wire rack to cool completely. Serve cut in thick slices.

Note: Store in an airtight container for up to 2 weeks. This loaf is also suitable to freeze.

CARROT AND HAZELNUT CAKE

SERVES 8–10

150 g (5½ oz/1 cup) finely grated carrots

165 g (5¾ oz/1½ cups) ground hazelnuts

70 g (2½ oz/¾ cup) dry breadcrumbs

a pinch of ground nutmeg

6 eggs, separated

230 g (8½ oz/1 cup) caster (superfine) sugar

2 tablespoons sweet sherry

ORANGE GLAZE

155 g (5½ oz/1¼ cups) icing (confectioners') sugar, sifted

10 g (¼ oz) unsalted butter, softened

2–3 tablespoons orange juice

1 Preheat the oven to 180°C (350°F/Gas 4). Lightly grease a 24 cm (9½ inch) round spring-form cake tin and line the base with baking paper. Dust the side of the tin with a little flour, shaking out any excess.

2 Put the carrots and hazelnuts in a bowl and mix to combine. Add the breadcrumbs and nutmeg and mix until combined, then set aside.

3 Whisk the egg yolks and sugar in a large bowl for 5 minutes, or until pale and thick. Stir in the sherry, then fold into the carrot mixture.

4 Whisk the egg whites in a clean, dry bowl until soft peaks form. Gently fold the egg whites, a third at a time, into the carrot mixture.

5 Spoon into the prepared tin and bake for 50 minutes, or until firm to the touch and a skewer inserted into the centre of the cake comes out clean. Leave to cool for 10 minutes, then remove from the tin and transfer to a wire rack to cool completely.

6 To make the orange glaze, combine the icing sugar and butter in a heatproof bowl, then add just enough orange juice to make a soft, slightly runny glaze. Place the bowl over a saucepan of simmering water and stir for 1–2 minutes, or until the mixture is smooth and glossy. Pour the icing over the top of the cake and smooth over with a flat-bladed knife or palette knife. Allow to set, then serve.

MARBLE CAKE

SERVES 6

1 vanilla bean or 1 teaspoon natural
   vanilla extract

185 g (6½ oz) unsalted butter, chopped

230 g (8 oz/1 cup) caster
   (superfine) sugar

3 eggs

280 g (10 oz/2¼ cups) self-raising flour

185 ml (6 fl oz/¾ cup) milk

2 tablespoons unsweetened
   cocoa powder

1½ tablespoons warm milk, extra

1 **Preheat the oven** to 200°C (400°F/Gas 6). Lightly grease a 25 x 11 x 7.5 cm (10 x 4 ¼ x 3 inch) loaf tin and line the base with baking paper.

2 **If using the vanilla bean,** split it down the middle and scrape out the seeds. Put the seeds (or vanilla extract) in a bowl with the butter and sugar and, using electric beaters, cream the mixture until pale and fluffy. Add the eggs one at a time, beating well after each addition. Sift the flour, then fold it into the creamed mixture alternately with the milk until combined. Divide the mixture in half and put the second half into another bowl.

3 **Combine the cocoa powder** and warm milk in a small bowl and stir until smooth, then add to one half of cake mixture, stirring to combine well. Spoon the two mixtures into the prepared tin in alternate spoonfuls. Using a metal skewer, cut through the mixture four times to create a marble effect. Bake for 50–60 minutes, or until a skewer inserted into the centre of the cake comes out clean. Leave in the tin for 5 minutes before turning out onto a wire rack to cool.

Note: This cake will keep, stored in an airtight container, for 3–4 days. It is also suitable to freeze. Cooling the cake on a wire rack ensures the base of the cake dries out and the cake does not steam in its own heat.

YOGHURT BANANA CAKES WITH HONEY ICING

MAKES 2 CAKES, EACH SERVING 8

180 g (6 oz) unsalted butter, softened

90 g (3¼ oz/¼ cup) honey

230 g (8 oz/1 cup) caster (superfine) sugar

1½ teaspoons natural vanilla extract

3 eggs

360 g (12¾ oz/1½ cups) mashed ripe banana — about 4 bananas

185 g (6½ oz/¾ cup) plain yoghurt

½ teaspoon bicarbonate of soda (baking soda)

375 g (13 oz/3 cups) self-raising flour, sifted

HONEY ICING (FROSTING)

125 g (4½ oz) unsalted butter

3 tablespoons honey

125 g (4½ oz/1 cup) icing (confectioners') sugar

1 tablespoon milk

1 Preheat oven to 180°C (350°F/Gas 4). Lightly grease two 15 cm (6 inch) round cake tins. Line bases with baking paper.

2 Cream the butter, honey, sugar and vanilla in a bowl using electric beaters until pale and fluffy. Add eggs one at a time, beating well after each addition, then beat in the banana.

3 Combine the yoghurt and bicarbonate of soda in a small bowl. Fold flour alternately with the yoghurt into the banana mixture. Divide the mixture evenly between the tins, smoothing the tops. Bake for 50–60 minutes, or until a skewer inserted into the centre of a cake comes out clean. Cool in the tins for 5 minutes, then turn out onto a wire rack.

4 To make the honey icing, cream the butter and honey in a small bowl using electric beaters until pale and fluffy. Gradually add the icing sugar alternately with the milk, beating well until the mixture is very pale. When the cakes are cold, divide the honey icing between the tops, spreading the icing to form rough peaks.

Note: These cakes will keep, stored in an airtight container, for up to 4 days. Un-iced cakes can be frozen for up to 3 months.

GREAT TASTES BAKING

BUTTERLESS RUM FRUIT CAKE

SERVES 12–14

310 g (11 oz/2½ cups) sultanas (golden raisins)

250 g (9 oz/2 cups) raisins

225 g (8 oz/1½ cups) currants

185 ml (6 fl oz/¾ cup) vegetable oil

125 ml (4 fl oz/½ cup) dark rum

125 ml (4 fl oz/½ cup) orange juice

230 g (8½ oz/1 cup) soft brown sugar

2 tablespoons treacle or golden syrup

½ teaspoon bicarbonate of soda (baking soda)

1 tablespoon grated orange zest

4 eggs, lightly beaten

185 g (6½ oz/1½ cups) plain (all-purpose) flour

60 g (2¼ oz/½ cup) self-raising flour

1 tablespoon mixed (pumpkin pie) spice

40 g (1½ oz/¼ cup) blanched whole almonds

80 g (2¾ oz/¼ cup) apricot jam, to glaze

1   Preheat the oven to 150°C (300°F/Gas 2). Lightly grease a 20 cm (8 inch) round cake tin. Cut a double layer of baking paper into a strip long enough to fit around the outside of the tin and tall enough to come 5 cm (2 inches) above the edge of the tin. Fold down a cuff about 2 cm (¾ inch) deep along the length of the strip, along the folded edge. Make cuts along the cuff, cutting up to the fold line, about 1 cm (½ inch) apart. Fit the strip around the inside of the tin, with the cuts on the base, pressing the cuts out at right angles so they sit flat around the base. Place the cake tin on a doubled piece of baking paper and draw around the edge. Cut out and sit the paper circles in the base of the tin.

2   Combine the dried fruit, oil, rum, orange juice, sugar and treacle in a large saucepan and stir over medium heat until the sugar has dissolved. Bring to the boil, reduce the heat and simmer, covered, over low heat for 10 minutes. Remove from the heat and stir in the bicarbonate of soda, then cool to room temperature. Stir in the zest, eggs, sifted flours and mixed spice.

3   Spread the mixture into the prepared tin and smooth the surface, then arrange the almonds over the top of the cake. Bake for 2 hours 15 minutes, or until a skewer inserted into the centre of the cake comes out clean (the skewer may be slightly sticky if inserted into fruit). Allow to cool in the tin.

4   Heat the jam in a saucepan over low heat for 3–4 minutes, or until runny. Brush the top of the cake with the jam.

Note: When storing the cake, cover the top with baking paper and then foil to keep it moist. This fruit cake will keep, stored in an airtight container, in a cool place for up to 1 month, or up to 3 months in the freezer.

ITALIAN CHRISTMAS CAKE

SERVES 18–20

440 g (15½ oz/1¼ cups) honey

60 ml (2 fl oz/¼ cup) red wine

235 g (8½ oz/1½ cups) blanched almonds, toasted and chopped

450 g (1 lb) glacé fruit (choose a mixture of citron, orange, pears, peaches and red glacé cherries), chopped into large chunks

410 g (14½ oz/3⅓ cups) plain (all-purpose) flour

115 g (4 oz/½ cup) caster (superfine) sugar

60 g (2¼ oz/½ cup) unsweetened cocoa powder

80 g (2¾ oz/heaped ½ cup) dark chocolate, finely chopped

¼ teaspoon bicarbonate of soda (baking soda)

½ teaspoon ground cinnamon

½ teaspoon ground nutmeg

a large pinch of ground cloves

1 teaspoon finely grated orange zest

1 teaspoon finely grated lemon zest

TOPPING

200 g (7 oz) glacé orange slices

30 g (1 oz) red glacé cherries

115 g (4 oz/⅓ cup) warm honey

1   Preheat the oven to 170°C (325°F/Gas 3). Lightly grease a 23 cm (9 inch) round spring-form cake tin and line the base with baking paper. Dust the side of the tin with a little flour, shaking off any excess.

2   Combine the honey and red wine in a small saucepan and heat, stirring often, over low–medium heat for 2 minutes, or until the honey has just melted and the mixture is smooth.

3   Combine the almonds, glacé fruit, flour, sugar, cocoa powder, chocolate, bicarbonate of soda, spices and citrus zest in a large bowl and stir to combine well. Pour in the honey mixture, then, using a wooden spoon, stir until a firm dough forms; it may be necessary to use your hands.

4   Transfer the mixture into the prepared tin and smooth the top. Bake for 60 minutes, or until a skewer inserted in the centre of the cake comes out a little sticky. Using the skewer, pierce the cake all over, decorate with the orange slices and cherries and then spoon over the warm honey. Return cake to the oven and bake a further 10 minutes. Allow to cool.

5   Remove the cake from the tin, leave to cool completely, then wrap in plastic wrap and store for 1–2 days before using. Slice thinly to serve.

Note: This cake will keep, stored in an airtight container, for up to 1 month. Glacé orange slices are available from some delicatessens and health food stores.

CHOCOLATE CHESTNUT ROULADE

SERVES 6–8

60 g (2¼ oz/1 scant ½ cup) dark chocolate, chopped

4 eggs

115 g (4 oz/½ cup) caster (superfine) sugar

100 g (3⅓ oz) tinned sweetened chestnut purée

60 g (2¼ oz/½ cup) self-raising flour, sifted

2 tablespoons hot water

unsweetened cocoa powder, for dusting

CHESTNUT CREAM

150 g (5½ oz) tinned sweetened chestnut purée

300 ml (10½ fl oz) thick (double/heavy) cream

1 tablespoon dark rum

1 **Preheat the oven** to 180°C (350°F/Gas 4). Lightly grease a 25 x 30 cm (10 x 12 inch) shallow Swiss roll tin (jelly roll tin) and line the base with baking paper.

2 **Put the chocolate** in a heatproof bowl. Sit the bowl over a saucepan of simmering water, stirring frequently until the chocolate has melted. Take care that the base of the bowl doesn't touch the water. Allow to cool.

3 **Whisk the eggs** and sugar in a large bowl for 5 minutes, or until pale and very thick. Beat in the chestnut purée and chocolate, then fold in the flour and water. Gently spread the mixture into the prepared tin and bake for 20 minutes, or until just cooked and springy to the touch (do not overcook or the cake will crack when it is rolled).

4 **Put a tea towel** (dish towel) on the work surface, cover with a sheet of baking paper and sprinkle the paper lightly with cocoa powder. Turn the cake out onto the paper, then carefully remove the baking paper from the base of the cake. Trim the edges to neaten. Using the tea towel as a guide, carefully roll the cake up from the long side, rolling the paper inside the roll. Put the rolled cake on a wire rack and leave to cool for 10 minutes, then carefully unroll the cake and cool completely.

5 **To make the chestnut cream,** combine the purée, cream and rum in a small bowl, then beat until just thick. Spread the cake with the chestnut cream, then carefully reroll, using the paper to guide you. Place the roulade seam side down and dust the top lightly with cocoa powder.

Note: This roulade is best eaten on the day it is made.

LEMON AND HONEY RICOTTA CAKE

SERVES 10–12

1 kg (2 lb 4 oz/4 cups) fresh ricotta
cheese (see Note)

175 g (6 oz/½ cup) honey

1½ teaspoons natural vanilla extract

60 ml (2 fl oz/¼ cup) lemon juice

finely grated zest from 2 lemons

½ teaspoon ground cinnamon

4 eggs, lightly beaten

35 g (1¼ oz/¼ cup) plain (all-purpose)
flour

poached nectarines or peaches,
to serve (optional)

1 **Preheat the oven** to 170°C (325°F/Gas 3). Lightly grease and flour an 18 cm (7 inch) round spring-form cake tin.

2 **Drain the ricotta** if necessary, then process in a food processor until smooth. Add the honey, vanilla, lemon juice, zest, cinnamon and eggs and process until well combined. Add the flour and pulse until just combined and the mixture is smooth.

3 **Spoon the mixture** into the prepared tin and bake for 1 hour, or until light golden and still slightly soft in the middle. Turn the oven off, open the door slightly and cool the cake in the oven. Put in the refrigerator to chill, then remove the cake from the tin. Serve at room temperature with poached fruit such as peaches or nectarines, if desired.

Note: Buy fresh ricotta cheese sold in a large block at the delicatessen. It has a much better texture than the ricotta cheese sold in tubs.

GUINNESS SPICE CAKE

SERVES 8–10

250 ml (9 fl oz/1 cup) dark beer such as Guinness

350 g (12 oz/1 cup) molasses

2 teaspoons baking powder

3 eggs

230 g (8½ oz/1 cup) soft brown sugar

200 ml (7 fl oz) vegetable oil

250 g (9 oz/2 cups) self-raising flour

2½ tablespoons ground ginger

2 teaspoons ground cinnamon

100 g (3½ oz/⅓ cup) marmalade

80 g (2¾ oz) candied orange peel quarters, cut into thin matchsticks (optional)

1 Preheat the oven to 180°C (350°F/Gas 4). Grease a 2.5 litre (87 fl oz/10 cup) kugelhopf tin and lightly dust with flour, shaking out any excess.

2 Combine the Guinness and molasses in a large saucepan and bring to the boil. Remove from the heat, add the baking powder and allow the foam to subside.

3 Whisk the eggs and sugar in a large bowl for 1–2 minutes, or until pale and slightly thickened. Add the oil and whisk to combine, then add to the beer mixture. Sift the flour and spices into a large bowl. Gradually whisk in the beer mixture until combined.

4 Pour into the prepared tin and bake for 1 hour, or until firm to the touch and a skewer inserted in the centre of the cake comes out clean. Cool in the tin for 20 minutes, then turn out onto a wire rack.

5 Heat the marmalade in a saucepan over low heat for 3–4 minutes, or until runny. Strain, then brush the top of the cake with some of the marmalade. Arrange the candied orange peel strips, if using, on top and brush with the remaining marmalade.

Note: This cake will keep, stored in an airtight container, for up to 7 days, or frozen for up to 3 months. Candied orange peel is available in thick pieces (about the size of a quarter of an orange) from specialist food stores and delicatessens.

WHITE CHOCOLATE, ALMOND AND CRANBERRY TORTE

SERVES 8–10

8 egg whites

200 g (7 oz) caster (superfine) sugar

250 g (9 oz/1¾ cups) good-quality white chocolate, chopped

195 g (7 oz/1¼ cups) whole blanched almonds, toasted, then chopped

200 g (7 oz/1½ cups) sweetened dried cranberries

40 g (1½ oz/⅓ cup) self-raising flour

1 **Preheat the oven** to 180°C (350°F/Gas 4). Lightly grease a 24 cm (9½ inch) round spring-form cake tin and line the base with baking paper. Dust the side of the tin with a little flour, shaking out any excess.

2 **Whisk the egg whites** in a clean, dry bowl until stiff peaks form. Gradually add the sugar, whisking well after each addition. Whisk until mixture is stiff and glossy and the sugar has dissolved. Put the chocolate, almonds and cranberries into a bowl, add the flour and toss to combine. Gently fold the chocolate mixture into the egg whites. Spread the mixture into the prepared tin and gently tap the base.

3 **Bake** for 1 hour, covering the cake with foil halfway through cooking if it begins to brown too quickly. Turn off the oven and leave to cool completely in the oven. Run a knife around the edge of the tin to loosen the torte, then remove it from the tin.

Note: The torte will keep, stored in an airtight container in a cool place, for up to 1 week. It is not suitable to freeze. Sweetened dried cranberries are sometimes seen labelled as craisins.

POLENTA POUND CAKE WITH BLACKBERRY COMPOTE

SERVES 6–8

150 g (5½ oz) butter

230 g (8½ oz/1 cup) soft brown sugar

115 g (4 oz/½ cup) caster (superfine) sugar

5 eggs

185 ml (6 fl oz/¾ cup) sour cream

¾ teaspoon almond extract

1 teaspoon natural vanilla extract

155 g (5½ oz/1¼ cups) plain (all-purpose) flour

1½ teaspoons baking powder

150 g (5½ oz/1 cup) polenta (cornmeal)

thick (double/heavy) cream, to serve

BLACKBERRY COMPOTE

80 g (2¾ oz/⅓ cup) caster (superfine) sugar

2 teaspoons lemon juice

500 g (1 lb 2 oz) blackberries

1 Preheat the oven to 180°C (350°F/Gas 4). Lightly grease a 24 x 14 cm (9½ x 5½ inch) loaf tin with butter.

2 Cream the butter, brown sugar and sugar in a large bowl using electric beaters for 2 minutes, or until pale and fluffy. Add the eggs one at a time, beating well after each addition. Reduce the speed to low and mix in the sour cream and almond and vanilla extracts.

3 Sift together the flour, baking powder and a pinch of salt. Add the flour mixture and polenta to the butter mixture and fold in. Pour into the prepared tin. Bake for 50 minutes, or until a skewer inserted into the centre of the cake comes out clean. Leave to cool in the tin for 5 minutes, then unmould the cake by running a knife around the inside edge to loosen. Turn out onto a wire rack to cool.

4 While the cake is cooking, make the blackberry compote. Combine the sugar, lemon juice and 2 tablespoons water in a saucepan, then stir over medium heat for 3 minutes, or until the sugar dissolves. Add the berries and stir to coat, then bring the mixture to a simmer. Cook over medium–low heat for 5 minutes, stirring occasionally, or until the berries are soft but still holding their shape. Cool to room temperature. Serve at room temperature or chilled.

5 Cut the cake into thick slices and serve toasted with the compote and cream.

COFFEE SYRUP CAKES

MAKES 6

1½ tablespoons instant coffee granules

90 g (3¼ oz/⅓ cup) sour cream

125 g (4½ oz) unsalted butter

165 g (5¾ oz/¾ cup) soft brown sugar

2 eggs

155 g (5½ oz/1¼ cups) self-raising flour, sifted

COFFEE SYRUP

2 teaspoons instant coffee granules

165 g (5¾ oz/¾ cup) soft brown sugar

1   Preheat the oven to 180°C (350°F/Gas 4). Lightly grease six mini 250 ml (9 fl oz/1 cup) rectangular tins, then lightly dust with flour, shaking out any excess.

2   Dissolve the coffee in 2 tablespoons boiling water in a bowl. Allow to cool, then add the sour cream and stir to combine well.

3   Cream the butter and sugar in a bowl using electric beaters until pale and fluffy. Add the eggs one at a time, beating well after each addition. Fold in the flour alternately with the sour cream mixture, then divide the mixture between the prepared tins and smooth the tops. Bake for about 25 minutes, or until a skewer inserted in the centre of a cake comes out clean.

4   To make the coffee syrup, combine the coffee, sugar and 170 ml (5½ fl oz/⅔ cup) water in a small saucepan and stir over medium heat until the sugar has dissolved. Bring to the boil, then remove from the heat. Spoon the hot coffee syrup over the hot cakes in the tin and allow to cool before turning out onto a wire rack.

Note: Coffee cakes will keep, stored in an airtight container, for 3–4 days, or up to 3 months in the freezer.

GREAT TASTES BAKING

STRAWBERRY ROULADE

SERVES 10

2 eggs

1 egg white

125 g (4½ oz/½ cup) caster (superfine) sugar

90 g (3¼ oz/¾ cup) self-raising flour

1 tablespoon caster (superfine) sugar, extra

250 g (9 oz/1 cup) smooth ricotta cheese

1 teaspoon natural vanilla extract

40 g (1½ oz/½ cup) icing (confectioners') sugar

250 g (9 oz/1⅔ cups) strawberries, hulled and chopped

1 Preheat the oven to 200°C (400°F/Gas 6). Lightly grease a 26 x 30 cm (10½ in x 12 in) Swiss roll tin and line with baking paper, leaving the paper hanging over the two long sides.

2 Using electric beaters, beat the eggs, egg white and sugar in a large bowl on high speed for 5 minutes, or until light and foamy. Sift the flour into the bowl and fold in quickly and lightly.

3 Pour the mixture into the prepared tin and smooth the surface. Bake for 8–10 minutes, or until the sponge springs back to the light touch. Lay a sheet of baking paper on a clean tea towel and sprinkle lightly with the extra caster sugar.

4 Turn the sponge out onto the sugared paper, remove the lining paper and, starting from a short end, roll up the sponge with the paper, using the tea towel as a guide. Cool for 30 minutes.

5 Mix the ricotta, vanilla and icing sugar together with a wooden spoon. Unroll the sponge and spread with the ricotta mixture, leaving a 2 cm (¾ in) border at the far end. Scatter over the strawberries, then carefully re-roll the sponge. Trim the ends, and cut into slices to serve.

FLOURLESS CHOCOLATE CAKE

SERVES 10

500 g (1 lb 2 oz/3⅓ cups) good-quality dark chocolate, chopped

6 eggs

2 tablespoons hazelnut liqueur such as Frangelico, or brandy

165 g (5¾ oz/1½ cups) ground hazelnuts

250 ml (9 fl oz/1 cup) cream, whipped

icing (confectioners') sugar, to dust

thick (double) cream, to serve

1 Preheat the oven to 150°C (300°F/Gas 2). Grease a deep 20 cm (8 in) round cake tin and line the base with baking paper. Place the chocolate in a heatproof bowl. Half fill a saucepan with water, boil, then remove from the heat and sit the bowl over the pan — don't let the bowl touch the water. Stir occasionally until the chocolate melts.

2 Put the eggs in a large heatproof bowl and add the Frangelico. Put the bowl over a pan of barely simmering water — don't let it touch the water. Beat the mixture with electric beaters on high speed for 7 minutes, or until light and foamy. Remove from the heat.

3 Using a metal spoon, quickly and lightly fold the chocolate and ground nuts into the egg mixture until just combined. Fold in the whipped cream and pour into the cake tin. Put the cake tin in a shallow roasting tin. Pour hot water into the roasting tin to come halfway up the side of the cake tin. Bake for 1 hour, or until just set. Remove the cake tin from the oven and cool to room temperature. Cover with plastic wrap and refrigerate overnight.

4 Invert the cake onto a plate, remove the paper and cut into slices. Dust with icing sugar and serve with cream.

SPONGE SANDWICH WITH JAM AND CREAM

SERVES 8

4 eggs

1 teaspoon natural vanilla extract

125 g (4½ oz/½ cup) caster (superfine)
sugar

60 g (2¼ oz/½ cup) self-raising flour

60 g (2¼ oz/½ cup) cornflour
(cornstarch)

2 tablespoons raspberry jam

300 ml (10½ fl oz/1¼ cups) whipped
cream

icing (confectioners') sugar, to dust

coloured cachous, to decorate

1 Preheat the oven to 180°C (350°F/Gas 4). Grease two shallow 20 cm (8 in) sponge tins and line each base with baking paper. Beat the eggs, vanilla and sugar with electric beaters for 5 minutes, or until pale and creamy — the beaters should leave a trail in the mixture.

2 Sift the flours together on a sheet of baking paper. Gently tip the flour into the egg and sugar mixture and fold quickly and lightly using a large metal spoon — do not overmix or it will lose volume.

3 Divide the mixture evenly between the tins. Bake for 20 minutes, or until a skewer comes out clean when inserted into the centre of each cake. Leave in the tins for 5 minutes, then turn out onto a wire rack to cool completely.

4 Spread one cake with the raspberry jam and whipped cream, then place the other cake on top. Dust with icing sugar to serve, and if desired, decorate with coloured cachous.

FIG AND RASPBERRY CAKE

SERVES 4

185 g (6½ oz) unsalted butter

185 g (6½ oz/¾ cup) caster (superfine) sugar

1 egg

1 egg yolk

335 g (11¾ oz/2⅔ cups) plain (all-purpose) flour

1 teaspoon baking powder

4 figs, quartered

grated zest of 1 orange

200 g (7 oz/1⅔ cups) raspberries, fresh or frozen

2 tablespoons sugar

whipped cream or mascarpone, to serve

1 **Preheat the oven** to 180°C (350°F/Gas 4). Cream the butter and sugar in a bowl until light and pale. Add the eggs and beat again. Sift the flour over the bowl and fold in with the baking powder and a pinch of salt. Chill for 15 minutes until firm enough to roll out.

2 **Lightly grease** a 23 cm (9 in) spring form tin. Divide dough in two and roll out one piece large enough to fit the base of the tin. Cover with the figs, orange zest and raspberries. Roll out remaining dough and fit it over the filling. Lightly brush the dough with water and sprinkle with sugar.

3 **Bake for 30 minutes,** or until the top and bottom of the cake are cooked. Poke a skewer into the cake to see if it is ready — there should be no wet cake mixture clinging to the skewer. Serve with cream or mascarpone.

Note: If fresh figs are not available, you can use the same amount of dried figs but you need to rehydrate them first. Simmer them in orange juice for 5 minutes until they are plumped up and soft.

YOGHURT CAKE WITH SYRUP

SERVES 8–10

185 g (6½ oz) unsalted butter, softened

250 g (9 oz/1 cup) caster (superfine)
  sugar

5 eggs, separated

250 g (9 oz/1 cup) plain Greek-style
  yoghurt

2 teaspoons grated lemon zest

½ teaspoon natural vanilla extract

280 g (10 oz/2¼ cups) plain
  (all-purpose) flour, sifted

2 teaspoons baking powder

½ teaspoon bicarbonate of soda
  (baking soda)

whipped cream, to serve

SYRUP

250 g (9 oz/1 cup) caster (superfine)
  sugar

1 cinnamon stick

4 cm strip lemon zest

1 tablespoon lemon juice

1 Preheat the oven to 180°C (350°F/Gas 4). Lightly grease a 20 x 10 cm (8 x 4 in) loaf tin.

2 Place the butter and sugar in a bowl and beat until light and creamy. Add the egg yolks gradually, beating well after each addition. Stir in the yoghurt, lemon zest and vanilla. Fold in the flour, baking powder and bicarbonate of soda with a metal spoon.

3 Whisk the egg whites in a clean, dry bowl until stiff, and fold into the mixture.

4 Spoon into the prepared tin and bake for 50 minutes, or until a skewer comes out clean when inserted into the centre of the cake. Cool in the tin for 10 minutes, then turn out onto a wire rack to cool.

5 Meanwhile, to make the syrup, place the sugar and cinnamon stick in a small saucepan with 185 ml (6 fl oz/ ¾ cup) cold water. Stir over medium heat until the sugar is dissolved. Bring to the boil, add the lemon zest and juice, then reduce the heat and simmer for 5–6 minutes. Strain.

6 Pour the syrup over the cake and wait for most of it to be absorbed before serving. Cut into slices and serve warm with whipped cream.

HAWAIIAN MACADAMIA CAKE

SERVES 10–12

375 g (13 oz/3 cups) self-raising flour

1 teaspoon ground cinnamon

375 g (13 oz/1½ cups) caster (superfine) sugar

90 g (3¼ oz/1 cup) desiccated coconut

5 eggs, lightly beaten

440 g (15½ oz) tin crushed pineapple in syrup

375 ml (13 fl oz/1½ cups) vegetable oil

100 g (3½ oz/⅔ cup) macadamia nuts, chopped

LEMON CREAM CHEESE ICING (FROSTING)

60 g (2¼ oz/¼ cup) cream cheese, softened

30 g (1 oz) unsalted butter, softened

1 tablespoon lemon juice

185 g (6½ oz/1½ cups) icing (confectioners') sugar, sifted

1 Preheat the oven to 180°C (350°F/Gas 4). Grease a 23 cm (9 in) round deep cake tin. Line the base and side with two sheets of baking paper, cutting it to sit 2–3 cm (1–1 ¼ in) above the side of the tin.

2 Sift the flour and cinnamon into a large bowl, add the sugar and coconut and stir to combine. Add the eggs, pineapple and oil and mix well. Stir in the macadamia nuts.

3 Spoon the mixture into the prepared tin and level the surface. Bake for 1 hour 15 minutes, or until a skewer comes out clean when inserted into the centre of the cake — cover with foil if it browns too much. Leave in the tin for 30 minutes before turning out onto a wire rack.

4 To make the lemon cream cheese icing, beat the cream cheese and butter in a small bowl. Add the lemon juice and icing sugar and beat until smooth. Spread over the cooled cake.

MADEIRA CAKE

SERVES 4

180 g (6½ oz) unsalted butter, softened

185 g (6½ oz/¾ cup) caster (superfine) sugar

3 eggs, beaten

165 g (5¾ oz/1⅓ cups) self-raising flour, sifted

2 teaspoons finely grated lemon zest

1 teaspoon lemon juice

2 teaspoons caster (superfine) sugar, extra, to sprinkle

icing (confectioners') sugar, to dust

lemon zest, extra, to garnish

1 Preheat oven to 160°C (315°F/Gas 2–3). Grease and flour a deep 18 cm (7 in) round cake tin, shaking out any excess.

2 Beat the butter and sugar with electric beaters until pale and creamy. Add the eggs gradually, beating well after each addition. Fold in the flour, lemon zest and juice until combined. When smooth, spoon into the prepared tin and level the surface. Sprinkle the extra caster sugar over the top.

3 Bake for 1 hour, or until a skewer comes out clean when inserted into the centre of the cake. Allow to cool for 15 minutes in the tin before turning out onto a wire rack. To serve, dust with icing sugar and garnish with lemon zest.

Note: This will keep for 4 days wrapped in foil.

PECAN AND ORANGE LOAF CAKE

SERVES 8–12

185 g (6½ oz/¾ cup) caster (superfine) sugar

140 g (5 oz) unsalted butter, softened

2 eggs, lightly beaten

100 g (3½ oz/¾ cup) ground pecans

1 tablespoon grated orange zest

185 g (6½ oz/1½ cups) self-raising flour

125 ml (4 fl oz/½ cup) milk

125 g (4½ oz/1 cup) icing (confectioners') sugar

1 Preheat the oven to 180°C (350°F/Gas 4). Lightly grease a 22 x 12 cm (8½ in x 4½ in) loaf (bar) tin and line the base and the two long sides of the tin with baking paper.

2 Beat the sugar and 125 g (4½ oz) of the butter with electric beaters until pale and creamy. Gradually add the eggs, beating well after each addition. Add the pecans and 3 teaspoons of the orange zest, then gently fold in the sifted flour with a metal spoon alternately with the milk. Spoon mixture into the prepared tin and smooth the surface.

3 Bake for 50–60 minutes, or until a skewer comes out clean when inserted into the centre of the cake. Leave in the tin for 10 minutes before turning onto a wire rack to cool.

4 To make the icing, place the icing sugar, the remaining orange zest and 1–2 tablespoons hot water in a bowl and mix until smooth and combined. Spread the icing over the cooled cake with a flat-bladed knife.

BEER CAKE

SERVES 4

125 g (4½ oz/1 cup) plain (all-purpose) flour
½ teaspoon ground cinnamon
750 g (1 lb 10 oz/3 cups) caster (superfine) sugar
275 g (9¾ oz) unsalted butter, chopped
3 eggs
500 g (1 lb 2 oz/4 cups) self-raising flour
120 g (4¼ oz/1 cup) sultanas
500 ml (17 fl oz/2 cups) beer
thick (double) cream, to serve

1 Preheat the oven to 180°C (350°F/ Gas 4). Grease a deep 25 cm (10 in) round cake tin and line the base with baking paper. To make the topping, mix together the plain flour, cinnamon and 250 g (9 oz/1 cup) of the sugar. Place in a food processor with 125 g (4½ oz) of the butter and combine.

2 Place the remaining butter in a large bowl with the remaining sugar and beat with electric beaters until pale and creamy. Gradually add the eggs, beating well after each addition — the mixture may look curdled but once you add the flour, it will bring it back together. Fold in the sifted flour, sultanas and beer.

3 Pour the mixture into the prepared tin and clump the topping together in your hands to form small balls, then sprinkle over the cake. Bake for 1 hour 50 minutes, or until a skewer comes out clean when inserted in the centre. Leave to cool in tin before inverting onto a wire rack. Serve with cream.

WALNUT CAKE WITH CHOCOLATE ICING

SERVES 6

185 g (6¼ oz) unsalted butter, softened

95 g (3¼ oz/½ cup) soft brown sugar

2 eggs

185 g (6½ oz/1½ cups) self-raising flour

90 g (3¼ oz/¾ cup) chopped walnuts

60 ml (2 fl oz/¼ cup) milk

CHOCOLATE ICING (FROSTING)

125 g (4½ oz/heaped ¾ cup)
  good-quality dark chocolate, chopped

20 g (½ oz) unsalted butter

1 **Preheat oven** to 180°C (350°F/Gas 4). Grease a 20 cm (8 in) spring form tin and line the base with baking paper.

2 **Place the butter** and sugar in a large bowl. Beat with electric beaters for 5 minutes, or until thick and creamy. Add the eggs one at a time, beating well after each addition. Fold in the flour and 60 g (2¼ oz/½ cup) of the walnuts alternately with the milk until just combined. Spoon the mixture into the prepared tin and smooth the surface.

3 **Bake** for 35 minutes, or until a skewer comes out clean when inserted in the centre of the cake. Leave in the tin for 5 minutes before turning out onto a wire rack to cool.

4 **To make** the chocolate icing, put the chocolate and butter in a heatproof bowl. Bring a saucepan of water to the boil, then reduce the heat to a simmer. Sit the bowl over the saucepan, making sure the base of the bowl does not touch the water. Stir occasionally to ensure even melting. Cool slightly, then spread over the cake. Sprinkle with the remaining walnuts.